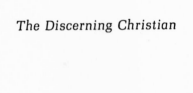

The Discerning Christian

The Discerning Christian

How the Believer Detects Truth from Error in the Midst of Today's Religious Confusion

by
K. Neill Foster

Christian Publications, Inc.
Harrisburg, Pennsylvania

Christian Publications, Inc.
25 S. 10th Street, P.O. Box 3404
Harrisburg, PA 17105

The mark of ℭ𝓅 *vibrant faith*

ISBN: 0-87509-312-4
Library of Congress Catalog Number: 81-69546
Quotations from the *New International Version* Copyright 1973
by the New York Bible Society International are used by permis-
sion.
Scripture quotations from the *New American Standard Bible*,
© The Lockman Foundation 1960, 1962, 1963, 1968, 1971, 1972,
1973, 1975, are used by permission.
Printed in the United States of America

To Marilynne,
The most discerning wife a man could ever have.

Contents

1

Purple Mountains

I was jogging with my dog as I am very much wont to do.

As I looked back over the broad expanse of the Beaverlodge Valley where we live, I saw the Rocky Mountains in the distance. Probably one hundred miles distant, they were purple in the morning light. And the early sun was sending slashes of gold onto the purple peaks.

The view was extravagant. Splendorous.

I had always been fascinated by those snowy peaks. And never had I seen them so magnificent. I was captivated again by those mountains that had always pulled my eyes to the southwest.

In my excitement I looked around for someone to share the view—someone to see what I had never seen before.

There was only my dog. Part Shelty they say. But not a very big part.

Impulsively I said, "Look, Abby! Look!"

He caught my excitement, canine that he is. His tail came up. His ears flicked forward. His black eyes seemed to sparkle with excitement. And the sensitive nose sampled the air.

He looked all around. Everywhere. Certain that a bird

or rabbit was near. Certain that he was on the brink of some stupendous dog-adventure.

The more I urged him to look at the mountains, the more certain he became that excitement was no more than fifty feet away.

Finally I realized that he would never see those mountains, ever, even though I am quite certain his eyesight is just fine.

A dog just does not have eyes for mountain splendors. He much prefers the sassy snarl of the neighbor's cat.

I realized then that I had the opening paragraphs for this book about Christian discernment, for it is, above all, about the Christian's ability to see much farther, to see much more than ordinary people do.

2

Christian Discernment

A. W. Tozer was fond of saying that the greatest need in the church was for the gift of discernment. And Dr. Tozer spoke from his perspective in the middle of the twentieth century. Were he able to comment on today's religious confusion, I am sure his tones would be more strident, his concerns still deeper.

It is certainly clear to Christian leaders everywhere that confusion is increasing. There seems to be a famine of clear thought and penetrating insight.

Robert H. Mounce, in an observant article in *Christianity Today*, says this:

> An educated person has also developed the power of discernment. We live out our lives in an atmosphere where truth and error constantly intermingle. If we are searchers after truth we accept the obligation to discern, to evaluate, to choose.[1]

And that obligation is what this book is about—developing the ability to be a discerning Christian in an age of confusion.

When we speak of Christian discernment, we refer to that special repository of penetrating insight and Christian wisdom that is the cherished heritage of the church. We refer to that ability from the Holy Spirit that enables godly men and women to slice through the surface confusion and to see the issues correctly and clearly. You are likely to discover as well an emerging and general definition of discernment as these pages unfold.

This Christian discernment involves, as we shall see, that special charisma of the Holy Spirit called the *discerning of spirits*, a special gift which only some Christians have. The special gift is discussed briefly in chapter 7; the general discernment is our subject everywhere else. All Christians may have discernment if they prayerfully apply biblical principles.

A biblical definition of this broad discernment is found in Paul's prayers for the fledgling churches in Ephesus, Philippi, and Colosse—all in Asia Minor.

> For this reason, ever since I heard about your faith in the Lord Jesus and your love for all the saints, I have not stopped giving thanks for you, remembering you in my prayers. I keep asking that the God of our Lord Jesus Christ, the glorious Father, may give you the Spirit of wisdom and revelation, *so that you may know him better. I pray also that the eyes of your heart may be enlightened in order that you may know* the hope to which he has called you, the riches of his glorious inheritance in the saints, and his incomparably great power for us who believe (Eph. 1:15-19a, NIV). (Italics added)

> And this is my prayer: *that your love may abound more and more in knowledge and depth*

of insight, so that you may be able to discern what is best and may be pure and blameless until the day of Christ, filled with the fruit of righteousness that comes through Jesus Christ—to the glory and praise of God (Phil. 1:9-11, NIV). (Italics added)

For this reason, since the day we heard about you, we have not stopped praying for you and asking God *to fill you with the knowledge of his will through all spiritual wisdom and understanding* (Col. 1:9, NIV). (Italics added)

For those churches and certainly for all the other assemblies of the New Testament era, Paul's obvious burden was that they should quickly develop that ability we are here calling Christian discernment.

For an Old Testament parallel, one might devotionally and reverently read the entire Book of Proverbs. When discernment is discussed there, reference is being made to the believer whose mind is steeped in the broad spectrum of practical advice in that ancient book.

If one wishes a specific Hebrew word to focus upon, there is no better one than *bene,* frequently used in Proverbs (1:5; 17:10; 17:24; 28:7) which means to separate, distinguish, consider, discern, perceive, and teach. But our overall purpose is not to focus upon a specific word. Instead, we must grasp discernment as the broad concept it surely is.

For those who crave a more precise definition of Christian discernment, let me say that I have chosen, carefully I hope, to build that definition gradually throughout these pages.

However, the discernment about which I speak is that insight, that wisdom, that understanding that enables a

Christian believer to see beyond what the natural man is able to see. All Christians have this discernment though obviously it is more highly developed in some than others. Also I must make clear, the special gift of discerning of spirits is not what is under discussion, although a few pages are given to it later.

This study touches a very deep need. In preaching and writing through this material a number of times, invariably I have seen keen interest exhibited in the ideas presented here.

We live in an age that cries out for Christian discernment, one in which men and women are looking for guidelines, searching for answers. By design, the answers probably will not all be found in this volume, but hopefully the standards by which all things may be discerned will be set forth here.

Finally, it is clear by Paul's letter to the Philippians cited earlier that the discernment about which he speaks and for which he prays has a very definite objective: spiritual maturity based on moral integrity.

I am persuaded that Christian discernment today will be identical to that for which the apostle so earnestly prayed.

---

1. Robert H. Mounce, "The Marks of an Educated Person," *Christianity Today*, November 2, 1979, p. 25.

3

The Philosophic Base

This whole idea of penetrating Christian insight rests on a basic supposition: *A biblical world view is the perspective for all real discernment.* Philosophy then becomes extremely important. The way a man looks at the world determines what he sees.

The humanist has elevated man to the throne. Man's good has thus become the essence of all real purpose in the world; the ultimate good has then become whatever seems to be good for man.

The hedonist has his philosophy, too. The flesh is all that matters. Beautiful bodies and orchestrated passions bring the real meaning to life. He must always be leering and selfish because his playboy philosophy causes him to look at this world through sensuous glasses.

The existentialist sees experience as the only reality. To him, all that matters is what he feels at any given moment. This philosophical system has made deep inroads upon modern thought.

The materialist (who may or may not be a Marxist) is required by this world view to discount Christian discernment immediately. He believes that the only things that are real are those which are seen or those things which can be felt.

The Christian, by his very nature, by his faith, believes otherwise. He looks at those things which are tangible and real, and he says, "All these things will pass away." The Christian believes the invisible is a reality and that it is more permanent than that which is seen and sensed.

So the philosophic base becomes very important here. There are a thousand philosophies, and they all might be discussed. They will not be, of course.

But the importance of philosophy to Christian belief can hardly be overestimated.

> The comparatively peaceful nineteenth century reflected the substantial unanimity of opinion and educational aims of western civilization. Particularly in Great Britain and America the prevailing philosophy was broadly Christian. People rather erroneously believed that God more or less directly governs the universe, and the curricula of American colleges usually culminated in a course in Theism. For over a century Bishop Butler's famous *Analogy of Religion* was a standard textbook, and toward the end of that era James Orr's *The Christian View of God and the World* became almost as popular.[1]

It is not difficult to surmise that the books by Butler and Orr are no longer popular due to the decline of Christian influence. Popularity, however, does not have much to do with truth. And if Christian truth has not changed, then these authors' ideas are essential even today. They certainly supply a philosophic base upon which Christian thought and discernment may safely rest.

But what did they postulate? What makes Orr's ideas,

for example, unacceptable to today's world? Below are listed the nine major statements that Dr. Orr felt would best summarize the Christian world view.

I. First, then, the Christian view affirms the existence of a Personal, Ethical, Self-Revealing God. It is thus at the outset a system of Theism, and as such is opposed to all systems of Atheism, Agnosticism, Pantheism, or mere Deism.

II. The Christian view affirms the creation of the world by God, His immanent presence in it. His transcendence over it, and His holy and wise government of it for moral ends.

III. The Christian view affirms the spiritual nature and dignity of man—his creation in the Divine image, and destination to bear the likeness of God in a perfected relation of sonship.

IV. The Christian view affirms the fact of the sin and disorder of the world, not as something belonging to the Divine idea of it, and inherent in it by necessity, but as something which has entered it by the voluntary turning aside of man from his allegiance to his Creator, and from the path of his normal development. The Christian view of the world, in other words, involves a Fall as the presupposition of its doctrine of Redemption; whereas the modern view of the world affirms that the so-called Fall was in reality a rise, and denies by consequence the need of Redemption in the scriptural sense.

V. The Christian view affirms the historical Self-Revelation of God to the patriarchs and in the line of Israel, and, as brought to light by this, a gracious purpose of God for the salvation of the world, centering in Jesus Christ, His Son, and the new Head of humanity.

VI. The Christian view affirms that Jesus Christ was not mere man, but the eternal Son of God—a truly Divine Person—who in the fulness of time took upon Him our humanity, and who, on the ground that in Him as man there dwells the fulness of the Godhead bodily, is to be honored, worshipped, and trusted, even as God is. This is the transcendent 'mystery of godliness' (1 Tim. 3:16)—the central and amazing assertion of the Christian view—by reference to which our relation is determined to everything else which it contains.

VII. The Christian view affirms the Redemption of the world through a great act of Atonement—this Atonement to be appropriated by faith, and availing for all who do not willfully withstand and reject its grace.

VIII. The Christian view affirms that the historical aim of Christ's work was the founding of a kingdom of God on earth, which includes not only the spiritual salvation of individuals, but a new order of society, the result of the action of the spiritual forces set in motion through Christ.

IX. Finally, the Christian view affirms that history has a goal, and that the present

order of things will be terminated by the
appearance of the Son of Man for judgment, the resurrection of the dead, and the
final separation of righteous and wicked
—final, so far as the Scriptures afford any
light, or entitle us to hold out any hope.[2]

Thus there is really only one philosophy in which
Christian discernment can function. I call it here the *biblical world view*.

To state this philosophy even more briefly is difficult,
but perhaps necessary. The biblical world view is just that
—a philosophy about the world based on the Judeo-Chris-
tian book called the Bible. This book alone is a sufficient
and inerrant authority in all realms. It is the repository of
inexhaustible truth; it clearly delineates right and wrong.
There is a God. A devil. Sin and hell. Heaven too. Justice
ultimately will be done. Jesus Christ is the Son of God, the
Savior of the world. He will return, and all history will cul-
minate in Him. The prophecies which described the events
in Jesus' earthly life as much as 800 years in advance also
made clear that one day upon His return the reins of all
human government will fall into His hand.

The biblical world view also regards the church of
Jesus Christ as an object of His special affection, the bride
which He is gathering to Himself. This worldwide fellowship of heart-believers is the church. Jesus Christ continues to build His church. And that church is at war with
the gates of hell.

Christian discernment rests upon this philosophic
base. Without it, there cannot be even rudimentary understanding of all that is about to be said. Within the biblical
world view, the Christian sees with startling clarity, with
amazing insight. His wisdom comes from God himself.

Little wonder that this Christian discernment is so

highly prized. No surprise that the wisdom of the world is always discarded at last.

---

1. Gordon H. Clark, *A Christian View of Men and Things*, p. 13.
2. James Orr, *The Christian View of God and the World*, pp. 32-34.

4

Some of the Issues

When one talks about current issues, he dates himself in the flow of Christian history since issues always change in the ongoing march of our Lord's church.

To date this book, to lock it into the last years of the twentieth century may be unwise, may undermine its usefulness in another generation. But the issues of today must be faced because they are what make us cry out so for discernment.

If our Lord tarries, there will be other issues in another day. But today, from my viewpoint, these are the issues—the movements and currents in evangelical Christendom which cannot be ignored. I also clearly identify myself as an evangelical Christian believer.

Ecumenism

Briefly stated, there is a worldwide urge in many segments of the Christian church somehow to forge the diverse elements of the church into one umbrella organization.

The Anglicans, for example, apparently cannot help but discuss a return to Rome. There are whole denominations such as the United Church of Canada, the Uniting

Church in Australia, and the United Methodist Church in the United States which by their names lend force to the conviction that all Christendom should be one. The World Council of Churches, formed in 1948 in Amsterdam, is the Protestant expression of this idea, and invariably cites the prayer of Jesus Christ as their proof text, "That they may be one, even as we are one" (John 17:22).

Those who hold the lower, more tenuous views of biblical authority are often those who are drawn to ecumenism. But there are those who implicitly believe the Bible, who fully accept its authority, who also tend to work toward the visible unity of the church.

There is another viewpoint that has an eschatological basis. The prophetic Scriptures warn that a pseudo-superman will rise, that he will be a religious figure. Some believe that this figure will come from the harlot church. And there are passages in Revelation which support this view. Any movement toward the church of Rome is then taken to be apostasy.

Those who resist the ecumenical movement tend also to believe that unity already exists among all true believers in Jesus Christ.

One exponent of anti-ecumenism put it this way, "I don't have a ripple of ecumenism in me." He believes that the unity of the worldwide body of Jesus Christ already exists. His viewpoint also includes the idea that there are intended to be differences of administrations and differences of operations within Christendom, and that there is no need at all to "get everything together." He believes the denominations in their diversities represent God's plan and purpose.

These two views and variations of them are in the church. What kind of spirit is at work? What is the mind of the Holy Spirit? The discerning Christian will know.

Success Ethic

America is the land of success. The Christian church has not escaped this influence, and as a result the largest churches, the biggest budgets, the most aggressive programs, the most effective evangelistic programs are often considered to be evidences of God's blessing.

But are bigness and power the real criteria for measuring God's blessing? Is the multi-national corporation really an expression of divine principles at work in the secular field? Are glass cathedrals and nationwide television specials the real symbols of successful Christianity? Is positive thinking always God's plan?

Inspirational leaders like Norman Vincent Peale and Robert Schuller have stimulated and encouraged millions. But the question must be asked, does not God sometimes have failure, brokenness, sickness, and even death in His plan?

The Americans, above all nations, have been a nation of doers. It can be done. Nothing is impossible. Is this attitude an outgrowth of the scriptural concept, "I can do all things through Christ which strengtheneth me," (Phil. 4:13) and "with God nothing shall be impossible" (Luke 1:37)? Has America led the world because of the heady optimism which has sprung from the religious idealism upon which the nation was founded? Or is this philosophy, once in the church, a twisted reality which ultimately disillusions all its devotees?

Church Growth

There is an outgrowth of the success ethic which has come to dominate missionary thinking worldwide. The leaders are men like Donald McGavran, Ralph Winter, and Peter Wagner—all associated now or in the past with the

School of World Mission in Pasadena, California. Other centers for the study of church growth are springing up in Deerfield, Illinois; Wheaton, Illinois; Regina, Saskatchewan; and elsewhere.

The Church Growth movement has an abounding literature, and basically has applied statistical methods, marketing techniques, and intense pragmatism to church growth. Methods have been discovered. Responsive peoples have been pinpointed, and churches have grown.

Interestingly enough, many evangelistic endeavors which once were examined as to whether they produced lasting personal conversions are now beginning to be examined by another standard: do these efforts result in church growth?

Is the Church Growth movement one of the most significant developments in the recent history of the church? Or is it simply an unholy philosophy which associates secular methodology with what is essentially the work of the Holy Spirit, the growth of the church? Has radical anthropology penetrated the movement, as Quebedeaux insists?[1]

Is there a departure from the truly biblical focus on Christ when methodological approaches are made to our Lord's Scriptures and to the church He is building?

Is a focus upon the *growth* of the church a dangerous tendency which deflects the church from proclamation evangelism to the studious application of those social sciences which are certain to increase the crowd? Is individual conversion being lost among the charts and statistical data?

Does the drive to grow threaten standards of holiness? Does it blur Christian distinctives such as the new birth?

Is everything that grows godly? What do studies about Mormons and Jehovah's Witnesses or anti-trinitarian groups have to do with the acts of the Holy Spirit in today's world? Is the Church Growth movement an unholy pragmatism or a fresh breeze of the Holy Spirit? Or is the truth somewhere in between?

The church of the New Testament was certainly a flourishing, growing church.

The worldwide diffusion of the Word of God is clearly expressed in the Bible. Many Scriptures can be summoned to substantiate the claim that our Lord's church is to grow.

Does the acceptance of growth as a criteria of God's blessing really vary from the convinced charismatic's appeal to supernatural phenomena as proof that his doctrine is correct? Is accepting tongues as an "evidence" of being filled with the Holy Spirit really any different from accepting growth as an evidence of God's blessing?

Yes, these are the questions, all valid, and the answers must be found. The discerning Christian will find them.

The Charismatic Movement

Today this burgeoning movement is worldwide in its scope and has penetrated every Christian denomination including the Roman Catholic church.

The teachings are diverse as well as consistent. Speaking in tongues has become the hallmark of the movement, the subjective evidence that the Holy Spirit is at work in the individual and the church.

Passages in Acts and Corinthians are cited as authority for the reception of such experiences along with the dramatic providences, miracles, and healings that accompany them.

Undeniably there has been a deepening of the faith of thousands. Millions have been won to Christ, and Pentecostalism in its denominational forms has planted churches around the globe.

The convinced charismatics usually attempt with the

zeal of a crusader to draw others into the ranks of the initiated.

But the charismatic movement shows an aversion to doctrine and an affinity to experience and providences.

As a result, and not surprisingly, the ecumenical movement has shown a deep interest in the "Pentecostal experience." This experience gets Baptists, Anglicans, and Roman Catholics on the same ground in a hurry. It does in minutes what years of doctrinal dialogue have failed to do. It unifies!

But there are questions. The more resolute evangelicals say that such manifestations are no longer to be in the church and that all present-day manifestations are either fleshly exhibitions or satanic delusions.

Still others add that pagan religions also have speaking in tongues. They fill the evangelical underground with true accounts of tongues demons being driven out in the name of Jesus Christ and of sexy, sensual, and phony Jesus-spirits which have affixed themselves to Christians who have frequented the charismatic milieu.

One evangelist affirms that in twenty years of evangelism involving exorcism and deliverance from time to time, one-third of the demons driven out has been pseudo-charismatic manifestations. Those who have reduced this finding to statistics affirm that of *those charismatics who seek counselling* on this issue, as high as 90 percent have spurious manifestations.[2]

Is the charismatic movement ultimately an unhappy mix of wheat and tares that is to be tolerated but hardly endorsed? With it, apparently, are found true evidences of the charisms of the Holy Spirit. But are all kinds of deceptions there as well?

Certainly it is impossible to be a thoughtful and sincere Christian in this day without having some kind of attitude toward the charismatic manifestations. Also, that this attitude should be a discerning attitude is immediately obvious.

Related to the charismatic movement is a phenomenon that is called "falling under the power." Apparently many people have fallen into trance-like states when in an intense charismatic atmosphere. Some evangelists have added "catchers" to the more ordinary need for ushers. And in some religious meetings, blankets are supplied so that supine women in varying degrees of immodesty can be covered. The Holy Spirit, it is said, has slain these believers.

In seeking to substantiate such phenomena from the Bible, many make frequent mention of the Apostle Paul, who was flattened on the Damascus road. Sometimes also the incident involving the guards who wished to seize Jesus prematurely in the garden of Gethsemane and were thrown backward is used as corroboration.

Others, of course, suggest that all is not as it appears. Occult subjection causes people to fall as well, they say. Incidents are related where evangelical believers have gone to such meetings while resisting all that is not of the Holy Spirit of Almighty God. In one cited case, thirty-nine people in a line of forty fell. Only the Christian brother who resisted all that was not from the Spirit of Almighty God stayed on his feet.[3]

In another case two evangelical pastors attended a service where "falling under the power" was a regular feature. They agreed to bind every spirit that was not the Spirit of God and to forbid all such exhibition unless motivated by the Holy Spirit of God.

That night there was no falling.

There are stories on both sides, of course. I have heard some of them myself. Many Christians testify to remarkable spiritual changes, to identification with Jesus Christ on His cross and more—all associated with what generally might be called "falling under the power."

Moreover, the history of revivals includes the record of similar phenomena. Charles G. Finney and Jonathan Edwards were famous for their tight logic, reasoned responses, and intense revivals. They also saw a lot of falling, though apparently the phenomena were invariably related to deep conviction of sin.

In the current scene, all kinds of views are propounded and all kinds of events take place, all in the name of Jesus Christ and the Holy Spirit of Almighty God. Is the falling phenomena occultism? Is it psychological deception? Is it one of the acts of the Holy Spirit today? Does it include some or all these elements? Or is it something else again?

Certainly only Christian discernment will ever sort out the answers here.

Christian Rock

These terms may seem to be mutually contradictory, and indeed they are since the word *rock* referred originally in black subculture to the act of fornication.

At the same time words take on new meanings, and Christian rock is now used to describe that type of music which takes typical rock-and-roll rhythms and adds Christian lyrics to them. The rationale is interesting too, since avant-garde evangelism has traditionally stolen the music of the world, adapted it to Christian words, and reached the masses.

General Booth, illustrious founder of the Salvation Army, could not see why the devil should have all the good songs. He proceeded to take beer hall songs, put evangelistic words to them, and stir the masses of his day. Are the rock-and-roll evangelists following in a long and honored tradition? Or has something sinister and new been added?

There are those who are convinced that music is a language in itself. Thus, rock-and-roll is a non-verbal expression of the immorality, perversion, and drug-orientation of the beat generation.

The immorality, debauchery, and homosexuality of the secular rock stars are cited, their frequent suicides tabulated.

Scriptures that speak about songs and hymns and spiritual songs are summoned to do battle with this gross evil.

It is remembered that Jeduthun (1 Chron. 25:3) prophesied in the Bible with an instrument alone, and that being so, the implication is clear that instrumentation and music alone have a message, without words. So again the question must be posed, "Is it really possible to use a medium of rebellion and sensuality to project a message of repentance and holiness?"

One of the biblical words used for praise means to "play loudly upon an instrument."[4] Music, or more specifically praise, can then be considered one form of non-verbal communication. *The music alone has a message.* Again a question must be asked, "Can non-verbal messages of rebellion and immorality be coupled with lyrics promoting repentance and holiness?" And if they are joined, what will be the effect?

Christian young people have tended to regard rock as their idiom, but the appearance of gay rock may be shaking that conviction.

The rock-and-roll evangelists may point to their crowds—nearly always large, and their converts many. "What we are doing must be of God. Look what is happening. We are just doing what evangelists have always done. Why should the devil have all the good songs?"

Still others cite examples where rock music has been played overseas and the native believers, recently delivered from spiritistic worship have asked, "Why are you calling the spirits?"

And of course there are the many shades of variation in between these extremes. Who will have answers for this confusion? Only the discerning Christian. Penetrating insight must be applied.

Christian Pornography

Again we have a clash of terms and ideas. Presently in North American publishing, two fields are booming. As might be expected, they are pornography and evangelical literature.

But can the two things be wed?

Something new has now been added. Christian publishers, in the interest of explicitness and saleability, have gone far beyond the terms of decency in publishing. All kinds of details about prostitution and perversion are being served up for the insatiable appetites of the reading public.

Not content with standards which would emulate the Bible, and the Bible certainly is frank and sometimes very earthy indeed, some evangelicals have pressed on to blasphemy, perversion, and explicit sex—all in the name of Jesus Christ, the building of the church, and the work of the Holy Spirit.

Probably the most shocking illustration of this trend is the publication of *Child of Satan, Child of God*. The co-author was one of the murderer Charles Manson's girls. She has almost certainly been dramatically converted to Jesus Christ. But in her book the inclusion of sensuous detail and the glorification of evil that precedes Christian conversion are unacceptable and naive. Or worse, plainly wicked. Should evil be published so that good may result? Presumably the Apostle Paul answered that question long ago (Rom. 6:1-2). And did he not say, "For it is shameful even to mention what the disobedient do in secret" (Eph. 5:12, NIV)?

Moreover, secular publishers are now developing evangelical lines. Can the world sustain the church? One of the main television networks in the United States now owns one of the famous evangelical publishing houses. Can sex and soap millions be used to beef up sales and bring back the King?

There may be those that say that editorial freedom is the answer and that if unbelievers' money can be used for the propagation of the Christian faith, fine and good. Others respond that believers are intended to be simple concerning evil (Rom. 16:19).

In the day when Christian books are judged by their four-color covers and their potential for impulse buying, what sells has become more important than what is right, biblical, or holy.

Christian books are everywhere today. C. S. Lewis and A. W. Tozer are available on the same stands as *Playboy.* Today's pagan will buy anything! So, apparently, will today's Christian.

Is this good? Or bad? Or is it a terrible confusion which mirrors the uncertainty of our day? Should certain Christian publishers be blacklisted for compromise and stupidity? Or should they be lauded to the skies for their brilliance and aggressive evangelism?

Simplistic, hurried answers are not enough. Surely there is no substitute for the profound wisdom and penetrating insight called Christian discernment.

Worldliness

Changes are more than apparent in this sensitive area of evangelicalism. Ever since the German pietists placed their indelible mark upon what is known today as the "born again" brand of Christianity, there has been a struggle in evangelicalism to keep its ranks "unspotted from the world" (James 1:27).

Christianity has, since its inception, implied a change in life style, a repentance, and an abandonment of the old way so that the new life might be embraced.

The separation Scriptures are well known, if not so often rehearsed these days: "Love not the world, neither the things that are in the world. If any man love the world, the love of the Father is not in him" (1 John 2:15).

Again the Scripture says, "Friendship of the world is enmity with God" (James 4:4).

Other texts can be summoned to buttress this idea.

But other strong evangelical minds discount the legalistic structures of the past. The Bible does not prohibit alcoholic beverages, just drunkenness, they say. Moreover, we should not live in an evangelical ghetto. We need to get out where the people are. Eat with them. We must not be fundamentalist Pharisees.

Television has done the most to break down the walls of separation. Burlesque shows that would have brought blazing shame a generation ago now march into the living rooms to produce evangelical titillation and "holy" giggles.

The religious movie now has a multi-million budget. Tickets at the door. Violence and innuendo in the text, and a gospel invitation (maybe) at the end. The evangelicals who a generation ago would have nothing to do with the "hollywood cesspool" now jam the theatres to the doors. And strangely enough, the movies of a generation ago were not always laced with immorality, homosexuality and perversion as they are today.

Christian movies are staged in local theatres. And when they are over and the smut is back on the screen, the little Christians never seem to notice. They just keep on trooping in.

A generation ago the late A. W. Tozer observed that inevitably the religious movie was gaining wide acceptance.

One thing may bother some earnest souls: Why so many good people approve the religious movie. The list of those who are enthusiastic about it includes many who cannot be written off as borderline Christians. If it is an evil, why have not these denounced it? The answer is lack of spiritual discernment.[5]

Are we asleep in Zion? The observation of the Lord's day has broken down. A generation ago when a baseball star refused to play on Sunday, he was a hero among Christians. Now football behemoths trudge to chapel first, and afterward out to trample the opposition.

Were the old times too strict? Today the preaching of Jesus Christ is penetrating society as never before. Evangelicals have burst out of their ghetto. They make their mark everywhere.

But does not the Book still say, "Without holiness no one will see the Lord" (Heb. 12:14, NIV)? Does it not say, "Let us cleanse ourselves from all filthiness of the flesh and spirit, perfecting holiness in the fear of God" (2 Cor. 7:1)?

Are evangelical gluttons to preach while Christian drunks are thrown out of church? Have God's laws changed? Or have evangelicals changed? Are we fooling ourselves while marching to this world's tune? The answers are not as clear as they seem to be. Could not a cloistered fundamentalist send as many people to hell as an evangelical libertine?

Peter Buckles, citing a survey taken by the Association of Evangelical Students, an affiliate of the National Association of Evangelicals, says this:

To determine which social habits they find to be acceptable, students at four Christian colleges were asked how they felt about six 'worldly practices' . . .About 60 percent felt that listening to rock music and social dancing would not compromise their Christian witness. Dating non-Christians, performing rock music, and drinking alcoholic beverages rated close behind, but were not as acceptable (40 percent). Students at all four schools rated smoking as least acceptable; 25 percent at one school felt it would not compromise their witness.[6]

Remember, these students profess to be evangelicals.

We must not ever forget that those who multiply negatives and encumber the Christian life with ever-louder "noes" are not strong Christians; they are by St. Paul's definition "weak" (1 Cor. 8:7). The weaker the believer, the more rules or borderline issues he is certain to have.

In such a milieu, where is the biblical voice that cries for true righteousness and holiness? Where is the prophet who can see as God sees, who can call pharisaical fundamentalists and worldly evangelicals to the same altar of brokenness in prayer?

Where he is, or if he shall ever be, we do not know. But if he comes, he will most certainly be a discerning Christian.

The Inerrancy Debate

There is something new in the kingdom—there are now out-and-out evangelicals who win souls, conduct aggressive evangelistic crusades, lead growing churches, and yet believe there are errors in the Bible. Historically, this has never been.

Harold Lindsell's *Battle for the Bible* was the unflinching book that crystalized the issues in America and brought the inerrancy debate to the fore. Lindsell believes that the admission of the possibility of error into the text of the Bible opens the door to all kinds of apostasy which is sure to follow.

In answer to Lindsell, Jack Rogers published *Biblical Authority*, a compendium of several authors, which, when carefully analyzed, is an appeal by errancy believers for a little maneuvering room in their dealing with the Bible. They appeal, not too convincingly, to history and seek to say that the church fathers were not such vigorous proponents of inerrancy as some think them to be.

The debate is hot and divisive. It is also so pervasive that no thoughtful evangelical can avoid the inerrancy controversy.

Is evangelicalism about to be divided, or is it already asunder? Is the debate about inerrancy a tempest in a teapot or the domino theory already activated in theology? Surely it is beyond the scope of this book or perhaps any other to give a definitive answer. Does apostasy inevitably follow errancy? Or will the controversy be forgotten as the immense task of world evangelization is tackled with energy and expertise never before available to the church of Jesus Christ?

The answers are not easy. Pragmatic foolishness may be as deadly as theological blindness. How can one know? How can one be sure?

As this book unfolds, as we probe this whole area of discernment, criteria from which answers may be derived will be forthcoming.

At this point, it is important only that the questions be raised.

Seducing Spirits

What do we mean here? It appears that Christians are being beset by all kinds of influences, and were the realities known, we would be agreed that these influences are seducing spirits.

The *family* and *personal faith* seem to be the two main areas under attack. Sex-triangles develop among Christian workers. Divorce is no longer just a problem in "the world." Divorce has marched, flauntingly, into the evangelical church.

Marriage partners are being pulled apart by all kinds of devious lusts. Fixations upon the opposite sex have become commonplace, and in the case of many believers, the seducing spirits proceed to set up all kinds of providences which lead the persons involved to believe that God is leading them away from their spouses. Women feel God is leading them to leave their husbands. Christian men feel God is providing the real love they have always lacked in their own marriages. But the fruits of these lusts are bitter indeed. God's children are seduced. Adultery and immorality usually follow. And divorce hard after.

Biblical teaching about the *agape* love which is commended for every marriage is sadly lacking.[7] The realization that love is willed and is to be followed by emotion is a concept that could save *every* marriage without exception. *Agape* love is love that springs selflessly from the will and does not regard feelings at all. This *agape* love, when exercised, triggers the feelings which follow.

The world's concept of feeling love has dominated the church. When feeling has gone, love is presumed to be gone as well. Then the seducing spirits are there with opportunities and providences galore. Often, too, they supply the wavering Christian with multitudinous scriptural texts, all of which seem to imply that immoral conduct is really God's magnificent plan.

Satan attacks the family because it thwarts his purpose in the world, because it is symbolic of Christ and the church, and because marriage is a power structure of oneness that he deeply fears. Once the home has been broken, all the family's defences are gone.

And what of the sects? Jim Jones's macabre exploits with his suicide cult in the jungle of Guyana are but one example of what is happening worldwide. To the clean-shaven Mormons, the persistent Jehovah's Witnesses, and the pseudo-intellectual Christian Scientists has been added in these latter days the politically oriented Moonies and the orange-robed Hare Krishnas.

What does one say about the thousands of sects floating around the periphery of Christianity? Is there not a Mormon spirit as surely as there is a Moonie spirit? Do not these seducing spirits all march to one tune?

Destroy the church.

Attack the church.

Destroy the church.

We are the only ones.

We are the only ones.

On and on the mournful litany goes.

Inquiring souls have been swept into the cults and reside in bondage still. Satan's army is not one bit diminished. The devotees simply switch from division to division in the army of darkness.

Seducing spirits are these. Sexual and religious. And a thousand other kinds. But always aligned against the church, always against Jesus Christ, the living God.

Samuel J. Stone, in his immortal hymn has caught the sound of battle and seen the triumph in the end.

The Church's one foundation
  Is Jesus Christ her Lord;
She is His new creation
  By water and the Word:
From heaven He came and sought her
  To be His holy bride;

37

With His own blood He bought her,
   And for her life He died.
Though with a scornful wonder
   Men see her sore oppressed,
By schisms rent asunder,
   By heresies distressed,
Yet saints their watch are keeping;
   Their cry goes up—"How long?"
But soon the night of weeping
   Shall be the morn of song.[8]

Emasculated Evangelism

In July, 1977, when Charles Colson, the convicted felon
of Watergate fame and author of a best seller called *Born
Again*, addressed the Christian Booksellers Association in
St. Louis, Missouri, he told the assembled book people that
forty million Americans professed to be born again and
that in his own endeavors and in those of many other evangelists, men and women were coming to Jesus Christ by the
thousands; and this he termed the good news. Then he said,
"Here is the bad news." He went on to chronicle the increasing lawlessness, immorality, and homosexuality in the
United States. Something, he implied is seriously wrong in
the most evangelized country in the world. People are, he
said, making decisions for Jesus Christ, but moral transfor-
mation is not following. There abounds, implied Mr. Colson, a form of godliness which denies "the power thereof" (2
Tim. 3:5).

What Mr. Colson summarized is that which millions of
Christians have come to feel. The contemporary declaration of the gospel seems to fail to carry with it the moral
revolution that almost invariably accompanied conversion
in the day of the celebrated revivalist Charles G. Finney, to
say nothing of the solid conversion that came under Peter's

preaching.

But then, say others, where does one see repentance in John 3:16? Are we always obligated to demand repentance before conversion? Does not the very word *believe* imply repentance? Is not the nature of the word *believe* such that it requires a person to turn from one thing to another? So the discussion goes on. The emphasis shifts to discipleship. The inquirers must be discipled for permanent conversions and lasting results.

Evangelistic and discipleship movements are to be commended, not denounced. Still, in all fairness, the questions have to be asked.

Is ours an emasculated evangelism? Has the heart of the gospel message somehow been glossed over so that we now proclaim a pale shadow of the truly apostolic message?

Or, as some surmise, is wickedness inevitably to increase, even though in the last days God will also pour out His Spirit on all flesh? Are we to expect godliness and wickedness to explode in tandem? Who has the real answers to these vital, vital questions?

Social Action

Increasingly these days, evangelical leadership appears to be embracing the political left. If in the past evangelicals have not always been Goldwater Republicans, they have definitely found themselves on the right side of the political spectrum. The reason has been easy to discern, too. Those who take the Bible seriously have been likely to be conservative in their political views.

But this is no longer the case. Evangelical Canadians now blithely vote for the socialistic, and not incidentally, humanistic New Democratic Party. In America, publications like *Sojourners, The Other Side, Radix,* and even "the evangelical *Mad Magazine*," *The Wittenberg Door* focus on social justice and the prophet Amos.

No one has documented this change in evangelicalism more adequately than Quebedeaux.

> As I said earlier, the vanguard of the evangelical left is centered on a small, highly literate, zealous, and generally younger elite, many of whose spokepersons helped formulate the Chicago Declaration. Evangelicals of the left range from moderate Republicans to democratic socialists, if not Marxists.[9]

Mr. Quebedeaux's entire text, *The Worldly Evangelicals*, chronicles the evangelical drift to the left.

Social concern has always been a byproduct of Christianity. And certainly that is not about to change. But the religious liberalism of the early twentieth century displaced evangelism with social action with disastrous results.

Evangelicals now are insisting still on the primacy of evangelism. They are in the words of John Stott, the elegant and erudite British spokesman for evangelicalism, prioritizing evangelism.[10] But Arthur Johnston suggests in *The Battle for World Evangelism* that evangelism has been dethroned.[11]

This is not the place for a full discussion of these issues. But does the increasing evangelical attention to social activism indicate the dethronement of evangelism? Is not any attention paid to activism certain to dull the evangelistic passion to win souls for Christ?

Does the evangelical drift to the left provide the certain evidence that biblical conservatism is being abandoned, that salvation by good works and social action will ultimately become an evangelical option?

Nothing less than broadly based and deeply rooted biblical knowledge will ever sort out the issues and answers here. Another name for that so desperately needed knowledge is discernment.

The concurrent move of some evangelicals to the far right cannot be overlooked in the consideration of the social action controversy. One of the most vigorous of these movements is the Moral Majority led by Dr. Jerry Falwell of Lynchburg, Virginia. He believes that Christian morality must be reestablished in America whatever the cost.[12] Falwell's agenda of moral priorities differs, of course, from that which might be offered by the publishers of *Sojourners*.

Feminism

The ordination of women is a popular media issue, probably second only to the popularity of reports on homosexual clergy. There are, however, increasing numbers of women in the evangelical fold who are embracing contemporary feminism.

Again, Quebedeaux's comments are precise.

> We have already seen that right and center evangelicals like Bill Gothard, Larry Christenson, and Marabel Morgan affirm the traditional subordination of women to men (in marriage, at least) by appealing to Scripture, taken literally. Former missionary and conservative evangelical author Elisabeth Elliot claims that the traditional man-woman relationship also reflects the submissive relationship of Christ to God. . .The roots of contemporary evangelical feminism—a movement within the evangelical left—can be traced back to Russel Prohl's book, *Woman in the Church*

(Grand Rapids, Mich: Eerdmans, 1957). Then came free-lance writer Letha Scanzoni's article in the February 1966 issue of *Eternity*, "Women's Place: Silence or Service?" advocating the ordination of women. Two years later she argued in the same magazine for the elevation of marriage to a partnership. In 1969 Scanzoni began corresponding with Nancy Hardesty, who was then teaching at Trinity College (Illinois), about the possibility of co-authoring a groundbreaking book on evangelical feminism—a work that was published finally in 1974 as *All We're Meant to Be: A Biblical Approach to Women's Liberation.*[13]

The evangelical feminists seem to be determined to accept only Galatians 3:28. Every other stricture on the ministry or activity of women in the church must be explained away.

Author Elisabeth Elliot, in *Let Me Be a Woman*, affirms, on the other hand, that "a woman can find true freedom only by submitting to the authority of her husband because in so doing she is really submitting to God himself."[14]

The Scriptures must be considered in this controversy, but the Bible scholars sometimes reflect their hermeneutical suppositions in the conclusion they reach about the meaning of Scripture. Such is the case with Paul K. Jewett when he concludes that St. Paul was simply wrong in what he wrote about the role of women.[15]

Others believe that women may certainly prophesy, or even be apostles (Rom. 16:7). The only biblical prohibition for their ministry is that they may not lead churches because a woman can hardly be the "husband of one wife" (Titus 1:6). Nor should women teach or usurp authority over men (1 Tim. 2:12). As a defence of this subordinate or complementary role, it is argued that such a role does not diminish personality nor equality with men. Are there not subordinate roles in the Trinity itself? The Father sends the Son. The Son sends the Holy Spirit. And to suggest that the Son or the Spirit are less than omnipotent, omnipresent deity is heresy.

Where do the biblical guidelines lie? What is the true role of women in the church? Is the submission of the wife to the husband in marriage a beautiful biblical pattern or an archaic remnant from ancient Jewish culture? Is the woman made for the man? Is the wife most fulfilled when she is most sheltered—protected by her husband?

The modern woman is looking for answers. And modern man would like to find them too.

And Finally

Many other issues could be raised. The ones I have chosen are set in the cultural context of evangelicalism in Canada and the United States in the nineteen eighties.

You will notice that the subjects have been dealt with quite evenly. Where this has not been the case you can attribute it to my bias or perhaps some small discernment gained in this study.

And of course, you will certainly want to add your own issues.

1. Richard Quebedeaux, *The Worldly Evangelicals*, p. 89.
2. K. Neill Foster, *The Third View of Tongues*, p. 89.
3. Wilbert McLeod, *Charismatic or Christian?* pp. 149-150.
4. James Strong, *Hebrew and Chaldee Dictionary*, p. 35, no. 2167.
5. A. W. Tozer, *The Menace of the Religious Movie*, p. 29.
6. Peter Buckles, "What Are Christian College Students Like?" *Christianity Today*, p. 29.

7. Foster, *Revolution of Love,* pp. 38-47.
8. Samuel J. Stone, "The Church's One Foundation," *Hymns of the Christian Life,* rev. and enl. (Harrisburg: Christian Publications, Inc., 1978), p. 395.
9. Quebedeaux, *The Worldly Evangelicals,* p. 84.
10. John R. W. Stott, *Christian Mission,* p. 35.
11. Arthur P. Johnston, *The Battle for World Evangelism,* p. 302.
12. Jerry Falwell, *Listen America!,* p. 23
13. Quebedeaux, *The Worldly Evangelicals,* p. 121.
14. Elisabeth Elliot, *Let Me Be a Woman.*
15. Paul K. Jewett, *Man as Male and Female,* p. 119.

5

Deception—A Fact of Life

The Bible, with which we are concerned, is replete with ancient examples of deception—that insidious, lurking factor in so many biblical scenes. In many cases, deception is the forgotten antagonist to Christian understanding.

In the third chapter of the Bible, Eve, the mother of us all, was seduced and deceived by the serpent. Into the pristine beauty of a new creation came sorrow and sin. Adam's sin was greater because he knowingly partook of the forbidden fruit; but Eve, as St. Paul makes clear, was deceived.

So creation was marred by deception. Lies and murder were soon to follow. Murphy's law had begun to operate: all that could go wrong did go wrong.

To seek to follow God and love Him is completely naive if one chooses at the same time to ignore the existence of a deceiver and the possibility of deception. And by implication, if there were no deceiver, then there was no need for the discernment that Eve simply did not have.

The Gibeonites

Not far into the Book of Joshua (chap. 9), the Gibeonites

perpetrated an exceptional ruse on Israel. Joshua had just led the Israeli army through the Jericho and Ai campaigns. The Israeli army was taking no prisoners, so the rest of the land trembled before it.

At that point, the Gibeonites disguised themselves with old clothes, dry bread, and shabby footwear. "We've come from a distant country"; they said, "make a treaty with us" (Josh. 9:6, NIV). Joshua and the elders did so only to discover that the Gibeonites lived right among them and that they had bound themselves not to destroy them.

So, just inside the promised land was deception.

In analogous thought, Christians have often considered Egypt as a type of the world, the wilderness wandering a type of struggle in the Christian life, the Jordan River a symbol of the experience of the fullness of the Spirit, and the promised land a symbol of life in the Spirit.

And one cannot help but notice, if we accept the typology, that as soon as the ongoing conquest of the promised land began, there was the confrontation with deception and a need for discernment which Joshua and the elders did not have.

The implication of the analogy is clear enough. In living the victorious Christ-life, one must expect to encounter deception. It is part of the walk in godliness. To focus on deception is, of course, unhealthy, but ignorance of it is deadly.

The Words of Jesus

In verse 15 of the seventh chapter of Matthew, the Savior pronounced some dramatic and unusual words. He announced the coming of false prophets who would prophesy in His name, cast out demons in His name, and do many miracles in His name; and further stated that He would reproach them for their words of iniquity (Matt. 7:22-23).

46

He made it clear that a good tree brings forth good fruit and a bad tree brings forth bad fruit. The prophets who have good character, who travel with their own wives, and who pay their own bills are the ones to be relied upon.

The preacher involved in an adulterous affair but still preaching and still winning people to Christ and still defending himself before his wife, is deceived. Good works do not a prophet make; nor do healings, deliverances, and miracles demonstrate that a prophet is a man of God.

We do not think that Jesus was setting Himself against the supernatural works He did and which He commissioned His followers to do.

But He was saying that one can know a man by his moral character. And one must never judge a man by the miracles he performs.

This may sound like heresy, especially in this existential, charismatic age. And indeed the convinced charismatics among us have more trouble with this passage than any other because it plays down the supernatural. It presents the possibility that many charismatic entrepreneurs are false prophets, workers of iniquity.

But one should not take an anti-supernatural position on the basis of these words. There are other Scriptures which make clear our Lord's desire to work miracles today. "'Have faith in God,' Jesus answered. 'I tell you the truth, if anyone says to this mountain, "Go, throw yourself into the sea," and does not doubt in his heart but believes that what he says will happen, it will be done for him. Therefore I tell you, whatever you ask for in prayer, believe that you have received it, and it will be yours'" (Mark 11:22-24, NIV).

Still the warning is inescapable. Miracles tend to deceive. And they will deceive the undiscerning.

John

The aged and beloved apostle has given to posterity and to the church one of the most dramatic passages on discernment to be found in the Bible. In 1 John 2:18-27 he refers to an anointing and to the antichrists who will precede the great Antichrist. Personally, so long as I presumed an antichrist to be only a political figure, I failed to catch the deeper meaning of John's written concern. But an antichrist is really, according to the meaning of the word, an anti-anointed one, or one with a false anointing. Antichrists, then, are religious figures with an anointing too, except that the anointing is false.

Now when one reads this passage through again, he sees that the contrast is clearly between a true anointing and a false or anti-anointing, remembering that the false anointing is no less real for being false. A false anointing is necessarily an action provided by Satan and activated through a demon spirit, even as a true anointing is an action provided by Jesus Christ through the agency of the Holy Spirit. When Jesus discussed false christs, he was describing those who are falsely anointed ones; John's antichrists are persons with a clear anointing, but an anointing which is *against* Jesus Christ, the Son of God.

The Greek prefix translated *anti* in John's writing also has another significant meaning, "in place of."[1] If one wishes to say that the antichrists John wrote about had a "substitute anointing," an anointing in place of the real one, he would not be doing a disservice to the text.

The implication of passages like these is not a comfortable one, especially for those groups in evangelicalism who pursue the "anointing" but tend to disregard or overlook moral qualities.

According to John, an anointing must be examined in view of its source. This kind of appraisal of spiritual anointings in our day would produce some fascinating and worrisome discoveries.

Undoubtedly the realization would dawn that there really are many among us with anti and substitute anointings! More on this later.

The Apocalypse

In John's revelation of Jesus Christ there are some interesting passages. In the thirteenth chapter, deception is accomplished by the use of miracles. The beast, later revealed to be the Antichrist, seduces the people with the prodigies and miracles performed.

In the nineteenth chapter, the beast and the false prophet are both hurled alive into the lake of fire because they have seduced *with miracles* the people who have actually received the mark of the beast.

Seduction in the scriptural world is best accomplished by miracles. And for those who are going to be discerning, miracles are things to watch; religious leaders also.

In the current history in which these lines are written the Iranian Revolution was begun and carried forth by a militant Moslem leader, The Ayatollah Khomeini. From Paris, with cassettes and spoken messages, he orchestrated a revolution that filled the streets of Tehran with millions of marching feet and toppled the two-thousand-year-old dynasty of the Shah of Iran. The whole city clamored for a man. A religious man, he proved in the end to be more powerful than any modern army could be.

Imagine, then, similar scenes in Boston and Bombay, Buenos Aires and Paris, London and Moscow, Tokyo and Washington, Jakarta and Los Angeles, Toronto and Mexico City. Imagine the populace in every nation marching and shouting for the same man. Only a religious figure will ever be able to accomplish a thing like that. The Antichrist, when he comes, will be a religious figure who will by Khomeini-like persuasion seize the reins of political power of the whole world. Plenty of supernatural acts can be expected. When a nation is to be deceived, miracles work best. When a world is to be deceived, miracles will be the tools to do the job.

Let us be clear at this point; we speak of the seductive, deceptive use of miracles. Christians should and do pray for the sick and see them healed. Humble Christians have prayed for the dead and seen them raised. There is no possibility of taking the Bible seriously and not believing that God is the God of the impossible. The promises of Jesus Christ make clear that the miraculous is to be a part of the church age.

> I tell you the truth, anyone who has faith in me will do what I have been doing. He will do even greater things than these, because I am going to the Father (John 14:12, NIV).

> Until now you have not asked for anything in my name. Ask and you will receive, and your joy will be complete (John 16:24, NIV).

But it remains true that the massive use of miracles will ultimately deceive all mankind. Who then will exercise discernment?

This section cannot be concluded without reference to *The Deceiver, Satan, The Devil, The Evil One.* There are many names for this angelic prince once called *Lucifer.* The first sin was his. Jesus testified that [in God's pre-creation world] He saw Satan fall from heaven like lightning (Luke 10:18). Eve was Satan's first human victim, but Adam followed forthwith. Jesus Christ resisted his overtures and persuasiveness. Instead, Jesus went about doing good and

50

healing all that were oppressed by him. Satan struck out at the cross. His final stroke against the Son of God became the Almighty's resurrection plan. Satan resisted Paul on his missionary journeys—in vain as it turned out. He has battered the church through the ages. He will lead one last failing rebellion against God Almighty and will be overthrown by the fire that comes down from God out of heaven (Rev. 20:7-11). His end is eternal torment in the lake of fire where the beast and the false prophet will be. The smoke of his torment will ascend upward forever (Rev. 14:11).

And Satan it is who is the deceiver. The demons and fallen princes who serve him in the world of darkness have a primary objective—the deception and destruction of the church. Incessant attack upon every Christian believer is the satanic battle plan; deception, the basic strategy.

---

1. See any Greek lexicon. *Antilutron (ransom)* in 1 Timothy 2:6 is a perfect example of the "in place of" meaning of *anti*.

6

Attitudes which Contribute toward Discernment

In approaching this whole matter of biblical understanding there are a number of factors which ought to guide us in our concern to develop the profound wisdom that is rightly called Christian discernment.

Get Your Sight

Spiritual life in Jesus Christ is the first basic requirement for discernment.

The Savior made it clear that unless a man is "born again" he may never hope to see the kingdom of God. Or put another way, a man remains spiritually blind until faith in Jesus Christ opens his eyes, enabling him to perceive spiritually.

Jesus had difficulty with His disciples in the eighth chapter of Mark. The disciples seemingly just could not comprehend what Jesus was doing. They had eyes, but did not see (v. 18). That is precisely the situation in the lives of many unbelievers today.

Twenty-twenty vision, physically, does not assure

discernment. Eternal life in Jesus Christ does bring it, though.

The blind man cannot and never will see until he receives his sight. After that, the life of discovery will unfold.

Ask the Question

In spiritual matters there often develops a strange paralysis among us. We Christians hesitate to question anything lest we grieve the Spirit of God, lest we contribute to dissension and division.

But actually God does intend that Christians have a questioning attitude. "Prove all things" (1 Thess. 5:21), and "Believe not every spirit, but try the spirits whether they are of God" (1 John 4:1), are both biblical injunctions not to be taken lightly. One is found right alongside the exhortation against quenching the Holy Spirit.

So I am saying we must stop accepting everything that happens in church as originating from the Holy Spirit. We must stop believing that everything done in the name of Jesus is necessarily authored by Him.

It is neither carnal nor unspiritual to ask the question. The failure to question will short-circuit the process of discernment.

Side with the Holy Spirit of Almighty God

There are many antichrists, said John (1 John 2:18). And Paul talked about "another spirit," so we must clearly take our stand on the side of the acts of the Holy Spirit of Almighty God in the world today.

The scriptural injunctions are clear. "Grieve not the Holy Spirit," and "Quench not the Spirit" (Eph. 4:30; 1 Thess. 5:19). There is a distinct danger that some of us may become so preoccupied with discerning that we fail to see the tremendous things God is doing in the world today.

An unprecedented evangelistic harvest is being reaped worldwide. Thousands of new churches are being formed in the nations of the world every week. Hundreds of colleges and institutions are training Christian leaders everywhere. The church of Jesus Christ is militant and on the march.

There will be groups of God's children who do things differently than we do. When long ago Jesus' disciples saw others working miracles and casting out demons, they wanted to forbid them. The Savior would not allow it. Instead, he said, "Do not stop him,. . .for whoever is not against you is for you" (Luke 9:50).

So it is today, there will be those who do things we do not understand, who behave differently then we do. But we ought always to side with the creative work of the Holy Spirit. We should fear to grieve or quench Him in these last days when God is pouring out His Spirit upon all flesh.

Cultivate a Wholesome Naivete'

This will appear to be contradictory because I have just quoted, "Prove all things." But love "believeth all things" (1 Cor. 13:7). Maybe it is contradictory. I happen to believe there are many things that the Bible teaches in parallel which are like the rails of a railroad. To insist on merging the rails, wrecks the train.

Christian discernment and wholesome openness are like that. Both can and should be cultivated. A wholesome biblical tension needs to be maintained. But if one falls into the suspicion syndrome, all one sees is deception. There seem to be demons under every tree; all Israel has bowed the knee to Baal, and we alone are left. This is not true today any more than it was true in Elijah's day.

If the Christian loses his disposition toward openness

and readiness to believe, he has lost a very great deal. This may not be a large section, but it is an important one. Openness must be preserved at all cost. *It is indispensable, and all discussion about discernment must not, dare not, destroy this precious quality of the Christian life.*

Recognize the Meaning of Confusion

The Scriptures assure us that "God is not the author of confusion" (1 Cor. 14:33). And the question may be immediately asked, who then is the author of confusion?

The answer to that is fairly easy, too. The possibilities are apparently only two: the devil and the flesh, meaning the carnal nature.

Billy Sunday is credited with this truism, and it is worth repeating. Said the bombastic evangelist, "I'm in favor of everything the devil is against, and against everything the devil is in favor of."

The corollary in this situation may be this, "I'm against all confusion because it almost certainly is from the devil or the flesh." It simply does not come from God, nor is it authored by Him.

To say further that all order comes from God would be going too far. Naziism was regimentation *par excellence.* The cults who deny the deity of Jesus Christ are often orderly indeed.

But confusion. Mark it always.

Think Carefully

There are a number of biblical injunctions directed to the mind, and though it certainly can be documented that much learning has made some people mad, God wants us to be mature in understanding—to allow the mind of Christ to dwell in us (Col. 1:27; 2:2-3).

There are some who suppose that after Creation the Almighty approached Adam from a blind side and dropped into his mind before he could protest.

Actually, Christianity produces magnificent, creative thinking. The biblical world view allows for all kinds of perceptive thought. The biblicist (though certainly not the materialist) understands the world as it really is. True education sharpens his mind and leads him always into more truth.

The discerning Christian must not despise the educational disciplines. He must recognize that reason and the ability to deduce logically are God-given gifts which quicken his mind and propel him toward greater understanding. At the same time he must not become so enamored of logic that he becomes incapable of believing anything that is not logical. Miracles are certainly not logical, nor is the doctrine of the Trinity. Still, concepts such as these must be believed.

To pursue education as an end in itself is the ultimate in foolishness. There are many professional students who are ever learning, but never coming to the knowledge of the truth. We do not speak of them. Their educational pursuits reveal their appalling lack of discernment. But the Christian who appreciates and welcomes the mental processes is likely to be a discerning Christian. True education is no less than residual discernment.

Those who rely on their feelings or senses to discern will falter here, but any kind of genuine knowledge, when viewed from the biblical perspective, will build wisdom and discernment.

That is why the Christian who would have wisdom and penetrating insight must not despise the way God has created him. An educated man may not be discerning, but a truly learned man certainly will be.

Keep the Church in View

Jesus said, "I will build my church; and the gates of hell shall not prevail against it" (Matt. 16:18).

One cannot read church history or travel the world as I have done and fail to realize that the church is "a-building" as it always has been. One marvels at its diversity. Tenacity. Durability. Doctrines first expounded two thousand years ago galvanize people into revolutionary action —and wholesome adoration—today!

It is true that the church has been beset by heresies and schisms, persecution and wars. Martyrs by the millions have motivated its march, and today the universal body of Christian believers, which I take to be the real church, is flourishing as never before.

Evangelism is vigorous in encounter. The doubters and cynics are simply being overrun by thousands of dynamic Christians, almost invariably evangelicals who clearly believe they have a job to do. Even the oldest denominations show some signs of life.

Now one of the key attitudes which will always aid in discernment is to ask the question, "What does this movement, this teaching, this idea do to the church? Does it build it up—or tear it down? Does it threaten it, divide it, or bless it?" When we are uncertain, when we wonder if this new movement or that is from God, we have only to ask ourselves one question, "Does this help to build the church of the Master Builder?" If it fails that test, it must immediately be questioned and its source impugned.

Some will disagree as to what does what to the church. The charismatic movement, for example, in the eyes of some is the key to revitalized, growing churches. In the view of superintendents and bishops it is often regarded with a very unfriendly eye. Whose criteria are the correct ones?

But I repeat, it is always helpful and safe to appraise any movement by what it does to the church. The long view may be needed. Creative tensions sometimes are for the good of the church.

But Jesus Christ is building. Building. Building.

And anything that does something else must be placed under scrutiny.

Expect Deterioration

"Evil men and seducers shall wax worse and worse," (2 Tim. 3:13). This is the biblical warning that multiplication of sects and heresies can be expected on every side. If Christianity has spawned a thousand different heresies, we can expect ten thousand in the future. More brazen. More bizarre. More diabolic. More destructive.

Before November, 1978, Jim Jones was an unknown lunatic with a few hundred followers. After the mass suicide in Guyana, his name was burned into the memories of literally billions of people, most often as an ugly example of Christianity run amok.

So we must not even be surprised when new religious maniacs arise. They will be controlled by even more powerful and abominable religious spirits. They will deceive thousands and even millions. The ravages will be such that the words of Jesus will come to mind, "When the Son of man cometh, shall he find faith on the earth?" (Luke 18:8).

We have not seen anything yet!

Monitor Holiness

"Without holiness no one will see the Lord (Heb. 12:14, NIV). Scripture urges Christian believers to be "perfecting holiness in the fear of God" (2 Cor. 7:1).

A great many discerning decisions can be made about a

great many issues by asking this question: Does this attitude, action, practice, or movement contribute toward personal holiness in the life of the believer? That single question will clarify many, many questions. That monitor on holiness will build discernment.

Cling to That Which Is Biblical

The tremendous need for biblical knowledge cannot be overstated, and all questions must be finally examined in the light of that which is thoroughly biblical. A knowledge of the Bible is the pulsating heart of Christian discernment. Berean Christians in New Testament times studied the Scriptures to see if those things St. Paul talked about were true (Acts 17:11). Discerning Christians in our day will be men and women of the Book. The more they know of the Bible, the more discerning they will be.

I would develop this theme here now, but in the section just ahead, we focus more fully on God's Word.

7

Channels of Discernment

Having come this far, we must now explain exactly how discernment comes. It is available. It *can* be exercised, and there are a number of clear channels through which Christian discernment comes.

There is some overlapping in the channels of discernment, much as one sees television channels sometimes overlapping one another.

But there are distinct channels for God-given insight.

Channel 1—The Word of God

We speak here of the Old and New Testaments, inspired by the Holy Spirit and completely and utterly trustworthy. The Bible, rightly and clearly understood, will solve all kinds of discernment difficulties.

The Scriptures plainly claim for themselves complete inspiration and freedom from error.

Every word of Holy Scripture is inspired or "God-breathed: (Gk. theopneustos). Without impairing the intelligence, individuality, literary style, or personal feelings of the human authors, God supernaturally directed the writing of

Scripture so that they recorded in perfect accuracy His comprehensive and infallible revelation to man. If God Himself had done the writing, the written Word would be not more accurate and authoritative than it is.

The inspiration of Scripture is attested by O. T. writers (2 Sam. 23:2-3; Isa. 59:21; Jer. 1:9) and by hundreds of instances where the expression "thus saith the Lord" or its equivalent is used. Christ affirms the inspiration of the O. T. (Matt. 5:18; 22:43-44; Mark 12:36; John 10:35). The apostles bear the same testimony (Acts 1:16; 4:24-25; 28:25; Heb. 3:7; 10:15-16; 2 Pet. 1:20-21). By means of divine inspiration the writers of Scripture spoke with authority concerning the unknown past, wrote by divine guidance the historical portions, revealed the law, penned the devotional literature of the Bible, recorded the contemporary prophetic message, and prophesied the future. Inspiration extends equally to all Scripture, although only a small portion was given by direct dictation of God (e. g. Exod. 20:1; Lev. 1:1; Deut. 5:4).

The inspiration of the N. T. was also authenticated by Christ (see John 16:12, note). The apostles claimed inspiration for their portions of the N. T. (1 Cor. 2:13; 14:37; Gal. 1:7-8; 1 Thess. 4:2; 15; 2 Thess. 3:6, 12, 14). Paul quotes both Deuteronomy and Luke as Scripture (1 Tim. 5:18; cp. Deut. 25:4; Luke 10:7). Peter declares all Paul's Epistles to be Scripture (2 Pet. 3:16). Although the N. T. sometimes quotes the O. T. loosely, in paraphrase, or interpretively, this is never done in a way to deny the authority or accuracy of the original text. The early apostolic church received the N. T. Scriptures as the inspired Word of God as they were written, though formal recognition of the entire canon came more slowly. Because the Scriptures are inspired, they are authoritative and without error in their original words, and constitute the infallible revelation of God to man.[1]

How to understand the Scriptures is also very important. The primary law of exegesis is appropriate here: "If the literal sense makes common sense, seek no other sense."

Further, all that one finds in the Bible is set in a meaningful context. That context simply must not be ignored.

Poetry is poetry even if it is in the Bible. There are passages in the Bible which are clearly allegorical, but simply to accept biblical literature for what it actually says is usually sufficient. As one person has observed, "It is not the things in the Bible that I do not understand that bother me; it is the things I do understand."

Idolatry, for example, stands so clearly condemned in the Bible that only literary fools could surmise otherwise. The Bible discerns.

The New Testament makes clear that a believing wife is not supposed to leave her unbelieving husband if he is content to dwell with her (1 Cor. 7:10-15). So if a wife receives a "word from the Lord" telling her to get rid of her ungodly husband, she knows, if she knows the Bible, that particular word is not from the Lord at all. The Bible has discerned, and knowledge of that Word has given the answer.

The Proverbs speak cautiously about a person who winks with his eyes and makes signs with fingers and toes (Prov. 6:13). People who carry on like that deserve to be under a question mark. And so far as the Bible is concerned, they are.

Lists of such things could be multiplied endlessly here, but the real point is that the Bible is unfailingly discerning. Undoubtedly, it literally has a million answers, and our recourse is "to the law and to the testimony" (Isa. 8:20). That is where we learn wisdom. That is where we become discerning. And no one who neglects or distorts the Word of God will ever be discerning.

Moreover, we could stop right here, and this message would be complete enough because a solid knowledge of God's Word is the primary and basic source of discernment.

New converts and untaught believers are often carried away into error simply because they are untaught and therefore easy prey for the enemy of their souls. The Bible literally opens men's eyes.

Channel 2—The Holy Spirit

The passages in John 14, 15, 16 make clear that the Holy Spirit has come into the world to be the divine Advocate and Guide for the church. It is His clear goal to lead Christian believers into "all truth" (John 16:13).

That being so, it is also clear that the Holy Spirit is in the business of giving wisdom and discernment to Christians. I have seen cases where the Holy Spirit has given biblical references or scriptural texts to persons in need of help. I have seen a demon-possessed person in desperation call out scriptural references unknown to her. One of the Christian workers would simply read the text, and a demon would be expelled by the reading of the text alone.

Preachers often have the experience of receiving additional insight and flow of material in the warmth and glow of biblical preaching. Some of this may be human enthusiasm alone, but most often, I believe, the Holy Spirit brings the extra dimension.

Who can doubt then that the Holy Spirit brings discernment? He needs to be recognized. Appreciated. Respected. He must not be grieved or quenched. He wants to fill and control the Christian. He wants to exercise the spiritual gifts through the believers. He wants to adore and exalt Jesus Christ. But He is the Spirit who searcheth the hearts, who knows all things. Because He is a Spirit, He communicates with the human spirit.

The ancients got "yes" and "no" answers from God. Since they did not possess a complete Bible, more direct means of consultation were used. A prophet interceded and received discernment and guidance by direct revelation.

In the New Testament age believers have the Word and direct access by prayer. In this day, some suggest, the inner witness from the Holy Spirit may be negative or positive according to God's will. In any case both Paul and John talked about the inner witness. And it is true, the Holy Spirit communicates directly to the human spirit. "The Spirit himself testifies with our spirit that we are God's children (Rom. 8:16, NIV). He will never deny the Word He has inspired, so all of us ought to know as much of the Bible as we possibly can.

But we have a marvelous Helper, too. The Comforter has come.

> Oh, spread the tidings 'round
> Wherever man is found,
> Wherever human hearts and human woes
> abound;
> Let every Christian tongue
> Proclaim the joyful sound:
> The Comforter has come!
> The Comforter has come,
> The Comforter has come!

The Holy Ghost from Heaven,
  The Father's promise given;
Oh, spread the tidings 'round
  Wherever man is found
—The Comforter has come![2]

And with His coming, penetrating Christian insight
and discernment have become possible.

Channel 3—The Body

The church is the Bride of Christ. It is also His body,
assembled and joined together by the Holy Spirit.
Ephesians 4 and 1 Corinthians 12 are the classic passages
explaining this mystical relationship in the kingdom of
God.

We are members one of another. And as the eye needs
the hand and the mind needs the feet, so the members of our
Lord's body are mutually interdependent. Since the gifts
are given severally as God wills and since no one has all the
gifts, an interdependence exists. The children of God need
each other, and they obtain discernment from one another.

My wife and I frequently interact this way. When one
has an idea or a proposal for a course of action we "bounce it
off" the other. We are looking for a reaction. Many times the
reactions will give us discernment.

The writer of the Proverbs put it this way, "In multi-
tude of counselors there is safety" (Prov. 24:6). And it is
true. Decisions reached which have been subjected to the
scrutiny of other minds are likely to be safer and saner
decisions.

In our evangelistic and publishing work we have an
Advisory Board which advises and consults. It is a sound-
ing board for new ideas, fresh directions. It is also a safety
device. Sometimes the members of our board josh that they

have brought their "rubber stamps." But not so. There are times when our Advisory Board brings the discernment of the body of Christ to bear upon our problems and deliberations.

And we are foolish indeed if we feel we have no need of others.

Some discussion of authority in the church is in order. The Scriptures teach that Christians should obey those that have the rule over them (Heb. 13:7, 17). This has been abused, of course, and some believers have been spiritually imprisoned by zealous overseers. But authority is a protective device. It allows the discernment of the body to have time and space to work. I personally have had and still do have Christian brothers over me in the work of the Lord. I do not find the relationship stifling. I find it protective— and helpful in discernment.

The spiritual gifts resident in the church contribute to discernment. Some spiritual gifts such as the word of wisdom and the word of knowledge are likely to contribute quite directly to Christian discernment, as is the gift of discerning of spirits which we shall discuss next. These gifts that contribute to discernment are in the body, and should one assume he has no need for the checks and balances the membership of the body brings into the life of a Christian, he is confused, if not deceived.

The discerning gifts, if allowed interplay in our lives, bring safety and protection to the body.

Conversely, to focus on one gift to the exclusion of all others creates a caricature of the gift. No one would want a nose a yard long or an ear that had to be tucked into one's pocket.

But when all is in order, the body provides discernment. We ignore it at our peril.

Channel 4—The Discerning of Spirits

This gift of the Holy Spirit has often been called the gift of discernment, but it is not that. It is the gift, the charism that enables one to discern *spirits* (1 Cor. 12:10). Admittedly, it is related overall to the penetrating insight we are calling Christian discernment, but the gift bears a direct relation to the spirit world. According to the Bible, there are at least four different kinds of spirits—the Holy Spirit, of course; the human spirit; angelic spirits; and finally, the fallen or evil spirits. The gift of discerning of spirits has to do with the intricate workings which take place in the spiritual world. A person with this gift should be more aware than other Christians of the action and interaction of these spiritual forces.

It should be clearly stated that the discerning of spirits is not a gift available to all. Some Christian believers have received it in the providence of God. It may be God's will for others to receive it since the gifts are divided severally as He wills.

One does not have the express statement that not all will receive the gift of discerning of spirits. In 1 Corinthians 12:29 (NIV), Paul did place a Greek negative before all his questions, "Are all apostles? Are all prophets? Are all teachers? Do all work miracles? Do all have the gifts of healing? Do all speak in tongues? Do all interpret?" For that reason the obvious answer in each case is no. But the implication so far as context and the basic meaning of the text is concerned is this: some have the gift of discerning of spirits, and some do not.

Since this discerning of spirits is also listed among the most supernatural of the gifts, I believe it is safe to assume that it tends to be supernatural in its manifestation. Rightly or wrongly, one tends to become acquainted with it in dramatic incidents.

I know a Christian brother who is remarkably gifted along this line. On one occasion when he stepped out of the car in front of a house where he had gone to visit, a woman bound by occult powers began to scream out in the back yard. Probably more accurately, the demons began to scream through the woman, "Get that man out of here. Get that man out of here!" The arriving evangelist could not see the woman at the rear of the house. Nor could the woman see who had arrived, but the demons knew. Just as the demons long ago knew Paul (Acts 19:15), they know some people today. They know especially those who are gifted with the discerning of spirits. The evil spirits are especially vulnerable before Christians so gifted, and they rightly fear them. Their domination of human victims is threatened by the function of this dramatic and wonderful gift in a believer.

More could certainly be said about this important gift, but that is beyond the scope of this book. What I have written elsewhere could be helpful to some.[3] I must add here that the discerning of spirits may be so sharp that the gifted will know the name and numbers of demons along with the specific methods needed for their expulsion.

I would like to underscore here, that there are some Christians endowed with unusual abilities, specifically, the gift of discerning of spirits. They have an extra dimension of discernment not available to all except in the context of the loving, caring, communicating body of Christ. Since the penetrating Christian insight under discussion here is that general wisdom which is clearly available to all discernment does not come exclusively through the gift of discerning spirits. To depend only upon a gift, often subjective in nature, available to only some of God's children, is unnecessary and foolish. But to ignore this important gift is the height of foolishness, too!

Channel 5—Experience

This will be surprising to some of my readers, but it is true nevertheless. Discernment comes by experience. That is why an adage "Experience is the best teacher" has had such a long life. "But solid food is for the mature, who by constant use have trained themselves to distinguish good from evil" (Heb. 5:14, NIV).

Discernment comes with time.

Trial and error. Age and experience. That is why Paul went about ordaining elders, not "youngers." That is why gray hair is one of the indications of discernment.

It is true that sometimes old men are fools; and there is no fool like an old fool. Age in itself does not assure discernment. But discernment comes with the exercise of the senses, and that takes time.

Why are senior pastors most conservative? Bishops and superintendents most cautious? There is a reason. It is not always discernment, of course, but sometimes, many times, it is.

Again the Bible demonstrates its reliability.

Channel 6—Patience

This section will not be lengthy, but it will be important. And it is related to experience as a factor in discernment. The passage of time itself clarifies issues.

In the United States, for example, the controversy over biblical inerrancy is intense at the present time. If the errancy proponents, as many believe, are really on a path of apostasy, ten years will clarify the issues.

The Scriptures are full of exhortations against haste and in favor of patience.

It is not good to have zeal without knowledge,

nor to be *hasty* and miss the way (Prov. 19:2, NIV). (Italics added)

But you, man of God, flee from all this, and pursue righteousness, godliness, faith, love, *endurance* and gentleness (1 Tim. 6:11, NIV). (Italics added)

You need to *persevere* so that when you have done the will of God, you will receive what he has promised (Heb. 10:36, NIV). (Italics added)

Our children often want us to make decisions in a hurry. But life is just not that way. Decisions taken in haste are often wrong.

Once when I had to make a very vital decision about offering a kidney to my dying cousin, my father said, "Whatever you do, don't do it in a hurry." Ultimately, my cousin received another kidney and two extra years of life as a result. The important factor was *time*. With it came discernment of God's will.

More recently, a friend in the United States phoned us at our publishing house in Canada. He needed thirty-five thousand dollars, and he needed it quickly or he would lose control of his distribution company for Christian books. I did not have the money to buy the shares he offered, but at the same time an interest in 1,400 Christian book racks all through the Southern United States would be interesting to any Christian publisher.

In discussion afterward, the concensus of two concerned friends was, "This is undoubtedly an opportunity, but we must not hurry."

Time proved that the man ultimately did not need to sell the shares, and he did not lose control of his company.

Time, vital time, allowed the issues to unfold and

allowed us to see the issues as they were.

Channel 7—Full Surrender

"Therefore, I urge you, brothers, in view of God's
mercy, to offer your bodies as living sacrifices,
holy and pleasing to God—which is your spiritual worship. Do not conform any longer to the
pattern of this world, but be transformed by the
renewing of your mind. Then you will be able to
test and approve what God's will is—his good,
pleasing and perfect will" (Rom. 12:1-2, NIV).

There is a very real sense in which abandonment to
God provides a large measure of discernment—so much so,
that I venture to say abandonment of oneself to God, to the
will of God, to the Word of God will certainly produce discernment.

The verb used in Romans 12: 1 and 2 is an aorist which
demands a once-and-for-all abandonment to God.

A parallel idea exists however in Ephesians 5 where
the Apostle exhorted, "Be ye not unwise, but understanding what the will of the Lord is. And be not drunk with
wine, wherein is excess; but be filled with the Spirit" (Eph.
5:17-18). And the sense there is "Be filled continually."

Personally, though I abandoned myself to God long
ago, I do not remember whether or not it was coincidental to
my conversion, though I think not. But it was done, and it is
still in force.

Still sometimes the words of the hymn seem to apply to
me, "Prone to wander, Lord I feel it." For that reason I renew
my vows to God. I ask Him repeatedly to fill me with the
Holy Spirit. Though I do not perform these actions to receive further discernment, I am beginning to realize that
these actions do result in discernment—discovering and

knowing God's will as experienced in these passages of Scripture.

I was born in Grande Prairie in the Peace River country of Alberta. My first encounter with the possibilities of full commitment to Christ came at the Peace River Bible Institute in Sexsmith, Alberta, a still flourishing, interdenominational Bible institute. There, it seemed, the speakers always challenged the young people to dedicate their lives to God, to surrender fully to God. Usually in those meetings we were asked to stand if we wished to signify our assent.

I remember that the young people stood row upon row. That we did it year after year, I now realize. As I look back in retrospect I realize that many of us who made that full surrender have been called into numerous fields of Christian endeavor.

In my own spiritual pilgrimage and ministry, I abandoned for a time the preaching of the idea of presenting our bodies a living sacrifice unto God. I did not disbelieve it; rather, I believed it to be an essential requirement for being filled with the Holy Spirit, an experience which I emphasized. In later years, I have come full circle. In our summer conferences now we tend toward a service somewhere in the schedule in which full surrender or renewal of those vows is our object and purpose.

We do not pursue these things for discernment's sake. We pursue them because we believe them to be right.

Further, I am persuaded that every Christian should abandon himself to God's will and that he should renew these vows from time to time. This is godly good sense.

This surrender also reveals God's perfect will. It brings the penetrating insight in Christian discernment we need so much.

When we abandon ourselves to God, we should be clearly giving ourselves to the God of the Bible who sent His only Son, Jesus Christ into the world and who manifests Himself in the person of the Holy Spirit today.

The Muslim who dedicates himself to Allah is misdirecting his devotion as is the careless charismatic who is allowing his senses to be orchestrated by a Jesus that may be sensual and antichrist even though apparently Christian. We must abandon ourselves to the Jesus Christ of the New Testament.

Channel 8—Godly Discipline

At the very heart of Christianity is discipleship; devotion to Jesus Christ is logically followed by appropriate disciplines. Not surprisingly, discipline sharpens spiritual discernment and insight.

The classic example is that of the Savior himself. As the Divine Son of God possessing all the attributes of God, there was probably no deep need for Jesus to be fasting when He was being tempted by the devil in the wilderness (Matt. 4:1-11).

Still, our Savior was fasting. Could He have seen through the satanic strategies without this extra discipline? Certainly. Of that there can be no doubt.

At the same time, His example is powerful indeed. Christians today who face crisis and temptation know that the meeting of these difficulties in holy discipline is clearly illustrated in the Bible.

Accordingly, we are saying here that holy and godly discipline is assuredly a channel of true Christian discernment.

Channel 9—Observing the Enemy

In some ways, I'm inclined to omit this section as I perceive it to be quite unusual though certainly not mischievous nor perverse.

Succinctly stated, I believe that sometimes we become truly discerning when we detect the activity of Satan, when we finally observe his direction and intent.

To be anti-devil is fairly good Christianity, even if it is back door theology!

When the Apostle Paul was being followed by a demonized girl who continually cried out, "These men are servants of the Most High God, who are telling you the way to be saved" (Acts 16:17, NIV), he finally turned on the devil. Apparently the enemy was caught like a rat out of his hole.

The demon was driven out. The fortune-telling ability disappeared, and the girl was delivered. Paul's actions, his discernment, followed a recognition of what Satan was seeking to do.

Probably I am sympathetic to this as well because on one occasion my wife and I discovered God's will in just this way.

In 1967 we were seeking God's will. We had sold our house, stored our furniture, and I had ceased taking evangelistic bookings. And while we waited we prayed.

One morning, as I drove to an early morning prayer rendezvous with a friend, I suddenly heard a voice. Whether or not this was audible I cannot say; real, it certainly was. The voice announced, "You cannot learn Spanish."

Apparently it was an answer. One of our options at that time was the study of Spanish. But later in the day as I pondered what had happened, I became more and more uneasy. And the Shepherd's voice I knew was neither spooky nor queer.

Finally the realization dawned, "That was Satan, not God." And logic brought me to a decision, "If Satan says I cannot learn Spanish, then surely I can, and I will."

The time for enrollment in a Spanish course had nearly

passed, so we phoned a missionary language school in Texas. Could we come, we wanted to know.

"No room" was their response.

Though there was initial distress, our hearts remained buoyant. Finally, I wrote to the language school to tell them we were coming anyway, room or no room.

The audacity of it shocks me today.

But before the letter had gone even a few hundred miles, we received a phone call over thousands of miles. There had been a cancellation. There was room after all.

So we moved our family to Texas. We studied the melodic language called Spanish. I became fluent enough to preach without notes, and in many of my years of ministry I have preached far more frequently in Spanish than in English. My wife and I have gone on to study French, and I have a preaching facility in that tongue as well.

Moreover, a whole cross-cultural missionary evangelistic ministry has opened before us.

And strangely enough, the key to discerning God's delightful and perfect will was finally discerning the maneuvers of the enemy.

My advice: Do not expect or seek discernment in this way. But it may happen.

Channel 10—Christ, the Living Word

The word of God is living and active. Sharper than any double-edged sword, it penetrates even to dividing soul and spirit, joints and marrow; it judges the thoughts and attitudes of the heart. Nothing in all creation is hidden from God's sight. Everything is uncovered and laid bare before the eyes of him to whom we must give account (Heb. 4:12-13, NIV).

This passage, so often erroneously applied only to the written Word of God, applies definitely to the Living Word of God: Jesus Christ, the Son of God. The personal pronoun used in Hebrews 4:13 clearly refers to a person, an all-knowing creature before whom everything is naked and uncovered: Jesus Christ, obviously.

Now He is also declared to be a discerner of the thoughts and the intents of the heart.

And, of course, when you think of it, we have come full circle. Christ is the secret of all discernment. His indwelling presence is certainly the key to understanding, wisdom, penetrating insight, and Christian discernment.

Little wonder that great men of God like Dr. A. B. Simpson became so enamored of the concept. "Christ in you, the hope of glory" (Col. 1:27). Christ is literally the total answer for every need in the Christian life.

Allow the Lord Jesus to dwell in you and manifest Himself through you, and you will share His holiness, manifest His faith, and demonstrate His discernment.

---

1. C. I. Scofield, ed., *The New Scofield Reference Bible*, (New York: Oxford University Press, 1967), p. 1,304.
2. Frank Bottome, "The Comforter Has Come," *Hymns of the Christian Life*, rev. and enl. (Harrisburg: Christian Publications, Inc., 1978), p. 144.
3. Foster, *The Third View of Tongues*, p. 65.

8

Discernment and the Will

The city was Bobo Dioulasso, Upper Volta, Africa. The hour was early as I stepped across the pebbled courtyard and into the Mission Chairman's residence. He was not there, but Jim Albright, the Mission Chairman from neighboring Mali, was. And since I was then involved in producing a first draft of this book, I asked him, quite naturally, "Is there anything you have to say about discernment?"

His response was immediate and beyond my comprehension.

"Discernment," he said, "must never be separated from the will."

But as the discussion developed and as I began to turn the idea in my mind, I began to realize that a most basic ingredient for this whole discussion of discernment had been supplied. In retrospect, I feel that one of the most important events in that African journey was that discussion on discernment and will.

Essentially now, let me explain how discernment and the will are related. There are often perceptive glimpses that come to us in life, penetrating Christian insights that come in moments of clarity. Almost invariably that insight requires a volitional response.

Sometimes the most difficult thing in all the world is to be still. But if a person received subjective discernment, private understanding and information about the needs of another, and silence is God's intent but the discerning person speaks, the discernment will decay in the basket. As soon as information which the Holy Spirit intended for one alone becomes public, the pearls have been cast before the livestock, and a judgmental attitude has been unleashed.

Let me illustrate. Let us assume a Christian brother with a highly developed gift of discerning of spirits recognizes that someone in a local assembly has deep demonic problems. The objective discernment may be completely accurate. But lacking self-control, the *will* to keep that information to himself, he begins to tell others about what he knows. Subjective discernment, when it goes public wrongly or prematurely, becomes judgmental and full of condemnation.

Discernment disintegrates when isolated from the Christian's Spirit-led will. There were times when Jesus our Lord saw fit to address the will, to urge men and women to be quiet about what they knew and what they had seen. That principle of silence is applicable today. When discernment is intended to be for one's understanding alone, uncontrolled speech is appalling. The will to silence is missing.

Again, discernment many times is objective in its purpose. That flash of insight from God is something which demands an active response—from the will.

An example known to me illustrates this well. In the Republic of Mali over forty years ago, an African heard the gospel preached. Instinctively, intuitively, he knew it was the truth that he ought to believe.

Instead of embracing Jesus Christ with his will, he turned to Islam. For forty years he followed Mohammedanism, knowing deep within all the while that it was false.

Finally, after rising in the ranks in his village until he had become the leading Mohammedan, he turned abruptly to Jesus Christ. Will, as always, was the key.

Another example. Let us suppose that a professor in a college or seminary sees that worldliness is creeping in, that devotion is eroded, and that errancy in the Bible is being embraced. What does he do? His discernment brings with it a dilemma.

He has tenure. A pension. Respect, prestige. It is much easier to be quiet. Not to rock the boat.

Rationalizations flood in. "Maybe things will change. Maybe I should wait. Are not Christians called to peace?"

His lips are sealed. He knows enough to start a revolution. But his will to act has abandoned him. He chooses the eroding status quo. And he muffles the alarms ringing from his conscience.

Or here is another hypothetical case. A publisher of Christian books receives a manuscript which he instinctively knows will sell. But it is unbiblical in certain parts, glorifies evil in other parts, and is clearly pornographic. True, there is a dramatic Christian conversion tacked on the end.

He knows better, but he wavers. He needs the money. But a "hot cover," an appealing title, and a complete marketing plan spring into his mind.

The book is published. Sales are immediate and large. The dollars roll in. Accounts of conversions come from every side. These he recounts with relish and publishes them profusely. Surely God is blessing this book.

But deep within he knows better. He really does know.

But his will was paralyzed when the contract was signed.

Surely one can see in this experience that the exercise of the will is essential to effective Christian discernment.

A final hypothetical case. An earnest Christian

becomes involved with the charismatic movement. Soon he realizes that the particular group with which he is involved is given to excess and extreme.

But the experiences are warm. His heavenly language makes him feel good. The prophecies sometimes bother him. They seem to be imprecise; or worse, they seem to strain biblical values. The interpretations of tongues also seem to be either unfailingly ordinary or queer.

Still there are healings. Dramatic deliverances. Breathless accumulations of providences. Often he hears the phrase, "This must be of God. Look how it worked out."

Then one day, in a moment of clarity, with his perception sharpened as perhaps never before in his life, he sees that his charismatic Jesus is "another Jesus" (2 Cor. 11:4)— a phony, sensual, deceiving Jesus. And he notices how rarely the full title of the Lord Jesus Christ has been used in his fellowship.

But his "tongue" feels so nice. The providences keep on multiplying. He just cannot bring himself to abandon something so pleasant.

His discernment is useless. It has been reduced to knowledge that will rise to judge him one day because his will was feeble, his conviction compromised.

The linking of discernment and the will is essential. Vital. Without it discernment is like the manna the morning after, rotted and full of worms. When afloat on spiritual wisdom and a surrendered will, Christian discernment is spiritual dynamite.

We should not be surprised that Jesus Christ summarized the whole issue clearly, centuries ago. "If any man will do his will, he shall know of the doctrine, whether it be of God, or whether I speak of myself" (John 7:17).

9

Discernment in the Book of Acts

The Book of the Acts of the Apostles, sometimes called the Acts of the Holy Spirit, is, not surprisingly, a discerning document. In a study of the text, I have concluded that there are at least forty incidents in this remarkable book where discernment is a factor in the flow of events.

Also, it seems appropriate at this point in our discussion to look at the events that surrounded the explosive beginning of the Christian church. The place of Christian discernment in those dramatic happenings created a fascinating mosaic.

Though the word *discern* does not appear in the English translation of the Acts, the effect and operation of discernment is strikingly clear.

And it is not surprising that discernment should be a vital part of the acts of the Holy Spirit in the infant church. But the appalling lack of discernment on occasion is very surprising, and we would find it incredible were we not accustomed to the Bible's habitual portrayal of people as they were.

Lack of Discernment

The lack of discernment surfaces quickly. In Acts 1:6

the disciples, after three years at Jesus' feet, after the trauma of the Crucifixion, and after the wonder of the Resurrection, were still asking if the kingdom might come then. Professor F. F. Bruce suggests,

> The question in verse 6 appears to have been the flicker of their former burning expectation of an imminent political theocracy with themselves as its chief executives.[1]

Casting lots for the choice of Matthias also seems to have been a strange manner for Christians to make decisions. We can surely be forgiven if we harbor doubts about the discernment of the disciples, especially in view of the fact that Matthias was never again mentioned in the Bible and that such a powerful apostle as Paul was about to appear upon the scene.

Later in 12:9, Peter was released from prison and apparently was not able to distinguish a vision from reality. The men of Antioch in 15:1 showed a critical lack of spiritual understanding when they said, "Unless you are circumcised. . .you cannot be saved" (NIV). And somebody surely lacked this precious discernment when Paul and Barnabas differed sharply over Mark in 15:39.

Paul's willingness to undertake vows, 18:18 and 21:26, seems to have been either a lack of discernment, or worse, a surrender to peer pressure. Some disagree, of course, and say that Paul was simply being all things to all men.

Probably one of the most difficult passages in the whole book is 21:4 where Luke perceived the Holy Spirit did not want Paul to go to Jerusalem. Yet Paul insisted on going. Paul knew prison awaited him, 20:13, and that he would not return, 20:25; still he persisted, impelled, it seems, to offer his life as a libation. Could the apostle have been too stubborn to be genuinely discerning? Have not the inerrant Scriptures invariably come through vulnerable and sometimes fallible men? Paul's humanness should not in any way be considered a detriment to his usefulness in giving to us his inspired writings. The facts are that all biblical writers were human, fallible instruments used by the Holy Spirit to fashion an inspired and inerrant book.

The apparent lack of discernment in the Book of Acts is an encouragement by helpful example. We today who make mistakes and fall into bad judgment can take courage. Even the apostles in the holy fire of the New Testament advance were sometimes dull, undiscerning, or even stubborn.

The Discernment of the Scriptures

Though we may attribute the dramatic insights of the speakers in the Acts to the vibrant inspiration of the Holy Spirit, I think it is also true that the leaders of the early church were given penetrating Christian insight into the Scriptures themselves. They were very discerning in their use of the Old Testament in the new age.

Peter's explanation of Pentecost is a classic illustration, and he turned it into a powerful evangelistic instrument. Stephen's rehearsal of the acts of God in the national history of his detractors proved so powerful that they leaped upon him to destroy him. Philip, in 8:30-39, seized a remarkable opportunity when he found an Ethiopian seeking after God and just coincidently reading the Book of Isaiah; he turned the event into effective evangelism, followed immediately by baptism.

Paul's preaching in the synagogue at Antioch may be an example of apostolic preaching to Jews. But it is also an example of the discerning use of the Old Testament to make clear that Christianity is not something new but rather the natural outcome of something that has gone before.

In 15:15, James couched his decision in the context of

83

the Old Testament (Amos 9:11, 12) so that when he resisted the Jews' efforts to impose the law on Gentile converts, he did so with their own Scriptures. And Paul in the closing section of the book, appealed to the Scriptures as his basis for going to the Gentiles. Not only would they listen, he said, but reaching the Gentiles had been God's mind all along (Isa. 6:9-10).

A study then of Christian discernment in the Book of Acts must not ignore the judicious use of Old Testament Scripture to launch the New Testament church. Interestingly too, all the main figures in Acts were quoted as using this powerful weapon, the Old Testament. It is as if Luke felt compelled to show that Peter, Paul, Stephen, and James all used the Old Testament to preach New Testament truth. They did so because they were discerning.

Discernment for Ministry

There are numerous dramatic interventions of the Holy Spirit in the lives of needy people in the Book of Acts.

At the temple gate (3:1-5), Peter seemed to know instinctively that this crippled man needed to be seized by the hand, helped to his feet, and commanded to walk. Peter later said to Aeneas before everyone, "Jesus Christ heals you. Get up and take care of your mat" (9:34, NIV). In this case there was no outstretched hand—only a brief command. But the result confirmed the method. With Tabitha, Peter put everyone out—perhaps to get rid of unbelief. Then again, he only spoke. But it was a creative word. The woman rose from the dead (9:40-41).

Always in the healing ministry Peter reacted differently. Significantly, in these cases, Peter did not anoint with oil, nor did he lay hands upon the sick, though he would have certainly approved of these measures. Trusting his discernment Peter approached each case according to the need.

Philip also had a healing and deliverance ministry as recorded in chapter 8. Particularly interesting is the reaction of the demons at Samaria; they left their victims, screaming as they went. Apparently Philip had discernment in its most specific and particular sense, the discerning of spirits. He knew the intricate working of satanic bondage, and the evil spirits were uncovered before him.

But Paul showed this basic discernment, too. The spirit-controlled girl, chapter 16, had been following him for days, announcing her underworld message. Suddenly, Paul wheeled and addressed himself to the spirit, "In the name of Jesus Christ I command you to come out of her" (16:18, NIV). The enemy was driven out. And immediately the owners of the slave girl, in a kind of perverse discernment of their own, realized that with the demon gone, fortune-telling powers were gone too, and they were angry.

Bruce's comments are helpful at this point.

> She is described by Luke as a "pythoness," i.e. as a person inspired by Apollo, the god particularly associated with the giving of oracles, who was worshipped as the "Pythian" god at the oracular shrine of Delphi (otherwise called Pytho) in central Greece. Her involuntary utterances were regarded as the voice of the god, and she was thus much in demand by people who wished to have their fortunes told.[2]

During his sea voyage to Rome, Paul's awareness of God's intent was also clear in his words to the fearful passengers as recorded in chapter 27. "Not one of you will lose a single hair from his head" (27:34, NIV) was his message. The mariners about to be shipwrecked were encouraged. For healing, exorcism, or the vital matter of survival at sea, the apostles ministered carefully, sometimes unpredictably, but clearly with discernment.

Natural Surprising Discernment

There are a few places in Acts where discernment appeared where it was least expected.

Gamaliel, the intervening Pharisee, had just the right words to save the apostles (5:34). Was it mere human wisdom, or was the insight from a higher source?

Simon, the supposedly converted sorcerer, after observing that after Peter and John had prayed for the believers they received the Holy Spirit, said, "Give this authority to me" (8:19, NASB). Peter censured and rebuked him severely, threatened him besides. But Simon's use of the word *authority* was not without significance. There appears to be here this perverse discernment to which we have already referred. In any case, the ministry of the Holy Spirit to the Samaritans was a ministry of authority, and Simon had clearly recognized that authority was involved.

The sons of Sceva attempted exorcism, too, with some discernment, but without vital Christian authority (19:14). Was this again the perverse or clouded discernment that even the sons of Adam sometimes seem to have?

Dr. Nevius, in his classic on the subject of demonic possession, offers that in China some seemed to exercise powers of exorcism even though they were clearly not Christians.[3]

There are different kinds of discernment. The natural man by keen observation and experience refines his perception to the point that he can make good judgments about many things. But human perception no matter how cultivated, has serious limitations. These examples of discernment in unregenerate men are on the level of natural discernment. They stand in vivid contrast to the enlightened discernment of those who walk with God.

Discernment, Will and Prejudice

The discernment of the Holy Spirit in Acts is apparent in its author, Luke. He wrote with graphic understanding, and from the point of view we are considering here, he frequently, very frequently, focused upon that penetrating Christian insight we have come to call discernment.

When there was need in the early church (4:34), there was discernment enough to know when property was to be sold and discernment enough to know when it was to be retained in private hands. Moreover, Peter seemed to have exceptional discernment in uncovering the deception of Ananias and Sapphira (5:1-11). This dramatic event accompanied by the judgment of death was so unusual that one wonders if even more than discerning was involved in it.

Lenski finds himself asking the same question:

> How did Peter gain such complete knowledge about the sin of Ananias? One answer to this question is found in 1 Corinthians 12:10 ". . .to another discerning of spirits." In the case before us, Peter had even more, namely the direct revelation of the Holy Spirit concerning Ananias and his wife.[4]

The answer, it seems to me, was that the Holy Spirit multiplied His working and added other divine gifts to Peter's penetrating discernment. When Satan's diversionary attack seemed about to pull the apostles away from the Word of God and prayer, the right decision was made.

When the disciples heard that Cornelius and the others had received the Holy Spirit as they had previously (11:17), they were satisfied.

When Peter explained his actions to the elders at Jerusalem (11:18, NIV), the elders had "no further objections." They had discernment that the Holy Spirit was at work.

When Barnabas, in a similar situation, headed to Antioch, he also discerned the evidence of the grace of God among the Gentiles. And "he was glad" (11:23, NIV). When this infant church at Antioch was devoting itself to the discipline of fasting and prayer (13:2, NIV), it was discerning enough to hear the Lord say, "Set apart for me Barnabas and Saul for the work to which I have called them." This was missionary endeavor in its infancy, and at its heart was discernment, the ability to discover the will and truth of God.

Luke's discernment surfaced again (13:6) when he called Bar-Jesus a false prophet. How did he know? Even if Luke had never seen Bar-Jesus, someone had had discernment. Paul too called him as he was. He addressed Bar-Jesus (13:10, NIV), "You are full of all kinds of deceit and trickery." Not everyone knows who is a false prophet, let alone what he may be full of. But Luke and Paul seem to have had no trouble.

When Paul and Barnabas related God's working among the Gentiles (15:12), the whole assembly at Jerusalem "became silent." That silence implies a sense of discernment about what the Holy Spirit was doing. When the apostles composed a letter to Gentile converts, it was "a masterpiece of tact and delicacy." And surely the reason is that the church was discerning. By recognizing the directions of the Holy Spirit they avoided schism.

When Aquilla and Priscilla heard Apollos (18:26), they discerned his partial doctrinal knowledge and judiciously invited him to their home so they might carefully teach him more about the Savior. That ordinary people were able to catch the attention of an orator like Apollos and then instruct him more fully is a tribute to their wisdom—and to his humility.

There are times, however, when discernment runs into the blank wall of stubbornness and prejudice.

Early in Acts (9:13) Ananias was afraid of Saul even though the Lord had given him a vision about Saul's coming. Did will or fear or even prejudice stand in the way? Three years later, the disciples were still afraid of Saul. Was it just fear? Or was there a hint of prejudice in their holding back the right hand of fellowship?

Peter's threefold vision in chapter 10 had as its purpose the preparation of the apostle and the church for a ministry to the Gentiles. Prejudice had to be broken down. Stubborn will had to be overcome.

The disciples should have been able to be discerning about God's purpose for the Gentile world without such visions. But iron prejudice and stubborn will short-circuited their perception, hindering their discernment. Even after Peter's extraordinary vision, the apostles in the early church had great difficulty accepting the fact that the Holy Spirit really had ordained that the gospel was to be sent to the Gentiles.

Lessons Learned

Luke's account has a teaching about Christian discernment that is most helpful. Who can help but be encouraged by the failure of even the apostolic elite to be discerning? Who cannot find hope in the appalling lack of discernment at some of the critical moments in the life of the early church?

There is help, too, in seeing how the Holy Spirit worked creatively. The ineptitude of the early believers ought to be an encouragement to us when we fail.

And there is a warning in this chronology of the Holy

Spirit. Discernment seems to have failed utterly when confronted with stiffened prejudice and the resolute will. Such failure is reason enough then to seek before God to be as pliable and unprejudiced before Him as it is possible to be, and reason enough also to say that the most important lesson on discernment in the whole Book of Acts is that prejudice and the stubborn will are larger threats to discernment than insensitiveness and ignorance will ever be.

1. F. F. Bruce, *The Book of Acts*, p. 38.
2. Ibid., p. 332.
3. John Nevius, *Demon Possession*, p. 10.
4. R.C.H. Lenski, *The Acts of the Apostles*, p. 196.

10

Apostle of Discernment

The Apostle John has become, for me, one of the most fascinating biblical writers. Clearly he had a special love relationship with the Savior. He referred to himself as the Apostle whom Jesus loved. Another has observed, "John leaned upon Jesus' breast—because He wanted to."

My view is that John came to be the Apostle of Discernment precisely because he was the Apostle of Love. Love, Paul explained, produces discernment.

"And this is my prayer: that your love may abound more and more in knowledge and depth of insight, so that you may be able to discern what is best and may be pure and blameless until the day of Christ" (Phil. 1:9-10, NIV).

A frequent visitor to our summer conventions has been Rev. Armin Gesswein of California. He has often urged his hearers to "go deep" somewhere in the Bible. That has found a response in my heart, and I feel that if there is one place I'd like to "go deep" it is in John's first epistle.

Some of the observations that follow here are the result of an intense desire to understand John.

That understanding cannot be realized apart from an overview of the scene in which John found himself. The Gnostics were battering the new church. The initial glory and power of Pentecost had subsided. Then came the back-wash; the church seemed caught in the undertow. False prophets and false doctrines were multiplying. The gates of hell had been let loose. Many of the apostles had been martyred. Perhaps John alone was left alive.

Under attack but unbowed, not defeated but in danger —that was the church in the latter years of century one. John, the perceptive apostle, was chosen by the Holy Spirit to record the Apocalypse. I believe he alone was perceptive enough among all the apostles really to see the future. And this same John addressed himself to truth and error.

While others will observe more here, I see John focusing in his first epistle on at least four important areas: true profession, true anointing, true discernment, and true love.

True Profession

True profession seemed eminently important to him. The express and written purpose of his epistle is found in chapter 5:13 (NIV), "I write these things to you who believe in the name of the Son of God so that you may know that you have eternal life."

He wrote to help believers know. He also wrote to help believers discern, to blow the cover off false professions. No less than thirty-nine times is *know* used in this epistle. That dominant emphasis is inescapable.

By chapter 2, after delving into the nature of sin and the necessity for walking in the light, John came down hard in verse 3. "We know that we have come to know him if we obey his commands" (NIV).

Some might think that this statement is the affirmation of the obvious. But there are literally millions in our day in North America alone who "believe" but who are apparently not at all interested in obeying. Satan's ancient strategy seems to be to separate faith and obedience. John was discerning enough to see that in his day. Whether we are discerning enough to see the same thing two thousand years later is another matter.

Another area John focused on is hatred and love. "Anyone who claims to be in the light but hates his brother is still in the darkness" (2:9, NIV). He was still talking about profession devoid of possession, observing that love is the proof of light. False professors can be spotted, John said, when their hate shows.

A love for the world is another "dead giveaway," so far as John was concerned.

> Do not love the world or anything in the world. If anyone loves the world, the love of the Father is not in him. For everything in the world—the cravings of sinful man, the lust of his eyes and the boasting of what he has and does—comes not from the Father but from the world. The world and its desires pass away, but the man who does the will of God lives forever (2:15-17, NIV).

Alarm over habitual sinfulness was still another warning flag that John hoisted. He said, "No one who lives in Him keeps on sinning. No one who continues to sin has either seen him or known him" (3:6, NIV). So, he concluded, "No one who is born of God will continue to sin, because God's seed remains in him; he cannot go on sinning, because he has been born of God" (3:9, NIV). The church of Jesus Christ would be far more discerning about false professions, false prophets, and false anointings if serious attention were paid to these criteria which John so carefully laid down.

He added at least one more aid to discernment (3:24, NIV); it is subjective in nature. "And this is how we know that he lives in us: We know it by the Spirit he gave us."

"We know that we live in him and he in us, because he has given us of his Spirit" (4:13, NIV). True believers will have the true inner witness of the Holy Spirit, and the false professors will not have it.

In Paul's writings, he described the work of the Holy Spirit thus, "The Spirit Himself bears witness with our spirit that we are the children of God" (Rom. 8:16, NASB). And he had earlier stated, "And if anyone does not have the Spirit of Christ, he does not belong to Christ" (8:9, NIV).

While I am not suggesting I have exhausted John's list of criteria for distinguishing between true and false professors, these areas are vital: obedience, love, separation from the world, practical holiness, and the true witness of the Holy Spirit. They were the things to look for in John's day. They are the things to look for today, too.

John's words are helpful in evangelism. Many a seeking soul has come to the Savior through them, but we must not forget that the primary reason for the epistle is to counteract error, to protect the church, and to sweep away the pretense of false professors, false prophets, and falsely anointed ones.

True Anointing

John proceeded to warn against antichrists (2:18). So long as we mentally associate all antichrists with *the* Antichrist, we will miss the point of John's warning. We will completely miss the whole thrust of John's words unless we see the religious aspect of the Antichrist.

A christ is literally "an anointed one." An antichrist then, simply, has an anti-anointing.

As we have said earlier, we must not say that the anti-anointing is phony. It is as real as it is possible to be. But it is an anti-anointing, a substitute anointing, a demonic anointing. It is against Christ and His kingdom.

Antichrists tend to be in the assembly (2:19). But they finally leave, and their leaving finally shows them for what they are.

You will notice John talked about the anointing of his children, an anointing which is "real, not counterfeit" (2:27, NIV). The real anointing teaches believers to abide. And the apostle could be assuming familiarity with chapter 15 of his Gospel here since one of its key passages (John 15:1-17) has to do with the absolute necessity of abiding. *At this point his epistle clarifies his Gospel. The Gospel says that abiding is essential. The epistle makes clear (2:26-27) that abiding and consequent fruitfulness come by an anointing which teaches believers to abide.*

The world will never understand personalities like Jim Jones and his suicide cult in Guyana or the aging Ayatollah Khomeini in Iran, who clung to power month after month when all the "political observers" felt sure he couldn't last. And surely there is no explanation for the power of these public figures unless one recognizes that there is an anointing that is real, but against Christ; spiritual, but against God; tremendously powerful, but satanically inspired.

The church needs to be reminded that there are "many antichrists" (2:18). They always start out from inside, but because their anointing is an anti-anointing they finally take a position against Christ.

There are *many* of them too. That would seem to indicate that only the discerning can detect those in the church with the anti-anointing. To see no antichrists today may be an admission of blindness. They are around, many of them.

Because the antichrist person is anointed, he will be influential, usually in a place of leadership. But he will finally be tripped up by his theology. He will deny the Father and that the Son, Jesus, is the Christ.

The real anointing, John concluded, will teach us, keep us from error, and teach us to abide.

Then he moved on to a more specific theme.

True Discernment

The discussion about antichrist led John naturally to the statement, "Do not believe every spirit, but test the spirits to see whether they are from God" (1 John 4:1, NIV).

It seems to me that only John could switch from talking about spirits to a discussion about false prophets without any sense of inconsistency.

John was able to see beyond the false prophet. He looked right past the human instrument involved, directly to the spirit at work.

The individuals through whom the evil spirits worked were practically ignored. The Apostle of Love just saw farther.

He also categorically stated that these spirits can be recognized. "Every spirit that acknowledges that Jesus Christ has come in the flesh is from God" (4:2, NIV).

This apparently simple statement, inspired by the Holy Spirit as it is, is a four-sided trap.

What the person involved might say was inconsequential to John. What the spirit said was all that mattered. He distinguished between spirit-speaking and natural human speech.

He also made it clear that a denial that Jesus Christ is come in the flesh is at once a declaration of falsehood.

But there is more. Silence on the part of the spirit involved is also an evidence of falseness.

And the verb, *acknowledges* is in a form in the original language which *demands* continual action.

In 1 John 4:2 and 3 the verb forms used indicate—

> that every spirit that *continually* and *genuinely*
> confesses that Jesus Christ is in the flesh is of
> God. Therefore reluctant admissions or occa-
> sional positive declarations that Jesus Christ is
> come in the flesh are not sufficient. *The confes-
> sion must be continual.*[1]

John, loving and discerning as he was, skirted a for-
midable pitfall into which all Christendom might have
fallen had he not been inspired by the Holy Spirit.

He said, "Do not believe every spirit." Universal questioning is in order. Healthy, godly skepticism is a Christian
virtue.

But he failed to say "Try *every* spirit." He simply said
"Try the spirits." The implication is to try some, not all. An
additional *every* at this point could have turned a loving
Christian church into a twisted party of witch hunters.

In 1 John 4:4-6, John said some things about listening.
The false prophet, the one with the anti-anointing, will *not
listen.* Antichrists *do not listen.* True believers listen to
John and to his words. Those not from God do not listen to
John.

This ability to listen is so important that John capped it
with the second major key text in his epistle: "This is how
we recognize the Spirit of truth and the spirit of falsehood"
(4:6, NIV).

Paul told Timothy essentially the same thing:

> If anyone teaches false doctrines and does not
> agree to the sound instruction of our Lord Jesus
> Christ and to godly teaching, he is conceited and
> understands nothing. He has an unhealthy
> interest in controversies and arguments that

result in envy, quarreling, malicious talk, evil
suspicions and constant friction between men of
corrupt mind, who have been robbed of the truth
and who think that godliness is a means to finan-
cial gain (1 Tim. 6:3-5, NIV).

Argumentativeness and constant friction give the false
prophets away. The anti-anointing produces quarrelsome-
ness and malicious speech.

True discernment ultimately is to know that a spirit is
speaking and to know whether or not Jesus Christ's incar-
nation is continually acknowledged.

True Love

I find it fascinating that in consecutive passages on the
anti-anointing and spirit-speaking, John felt it necessary to
plunge immediately into a discourse on love. If my premise
about this chapter is correct, John had to arrive at love. He
had no other choice. His loving heart alone provided the
sensitivity and discernment which enabled him to deal
with the antichrists and false prophets.

In fact closer observation shows that John's most
probing teaching on discernment is literally sandwiched
between love passages.

3:11-24—Love Passage
4:1-6—Discernment Passage
4:7—5:3—Love Passage

To exhaust John's teaching on love will not ever be accomplished by any writer, much less can it be condensed
to provide a part of one chapter here.

But I must observe that God's love flows. The word
used in verse 7 of chapter 4, *comes*, implies this flow.

The nature of divine love is reflected in the word *choice*. Love is contagious; it runs from one to another; it explodes. Our Lord has literally shed it abroad into our hearts by the Holy Ghost (Rom. 5:5).

On the climactic Saturday of the Nakamun summer convention of 1971 through the ministry of Argentine evangelist Carmelo Terranova, all who were present will never forget, ever, that God's love was washing over the rolling contours of the Nakamun grounds in Northern Alberta. We were swimming in it. When the Canadian revival later exploded in Saskatchewan and the word went out, "We are knee deep in love," we understood.

In the days of that revival, 1971-1972, whole congregations learned to discern—how could they help but do so in a movement which gushed love?

The Apostle John was not oblivious to this quality inherent in love. And since logic cooperates with the inspiration of the Holy Spirit, he had no other choice than to counter the gnostic threat with love-discernment teaching.

John also used the phrase, "Love is made complete" (vv. 12, 17, NIV). This statement twice repeated reflects great importance.

Sociologists suggest that man has two very basic needs, to love and to be loved. If you will, love requires completion. It finds fulfillment in completion and response.

There are no Scriptures which directly say that women are to love their husbands. But there is the exhortation, "Teach the young women. . .to love their husbands. . ." (Titus 2:4).

Love, then, is something which can be taught. The fascinating thing for me here has been to discover that the passage has an implied meaning which is completely captivating. "Teach the younger women to *respond* in love to their husbands."

The husband is to love. He is the initiator.

The wife is to respond. She is the responder!! There is the urge to complete. God's love is completed in us. And our love is completed in Him.

Love is surpassingly important. It craves completion. *It is the womb of developing discernment.*

John also said, "So we know and rely on the love God has for us" (4:16, NIV).

God's love was known and therefore deemed to be reliable. Indeed, one might write "discern" every time John used "know" (thirty-nine times in the epistle) and not do an injustice to the Scripture.

This passage suggests also the possibility of spurious love. It has been often said, "Satan cannot imitate love." But he surely does, though it should more correctly be called lust.

Again, there are constant biblical injunctions to couple love with obedience. Apparently even in New Testament times there existed a "no-obedience" brand of love.

In Chile I remember being in a service where the leader decided to encourage all present to go from one to the other, (abrazandonos) embracing one another. Essentially I agree with the idea that love needs to be expressed. I often have preached about it and have written a book about it as well.[2] Still, I was appalled. I wanted to run out of the building. There was something wrong.

While addressing college students in another situation, some of the young men seemed to want to respond to my message about love by embracing the young women, especially the most shapely ones. Again I was shocked.

Later my considered conclusion in both those cases was this: heart cleansing needs to precede and to be vitally associated with expressions of love. Otherwise that love may easily become twisted, grotesque. And Peter had said it first, "See that ye love one another with a pure heart fervently" (1 Pet. 1:22).

John knew true and false love. He was discerning enough to insist repeatedly in the first epistle and elsewhere that love always is associated with obedience. "This is how we know that we love the children of God: by loving God and carrying out his commands" (1 John 5:2, NIV).

So, we are here saying, John's loving spirit, his intense love for the Master, his grasp and expression of the theology of love uniquely equipped him for the exercise of true discernment. He was the Apostle of Discernment precisely because he was the Apostle of Love.

This whole book then can be concluded with the words of another Apostle, Paul.

"And now these three remain: faith, hope and love. But the greatest of these is love," (1 Cor. 13:13, NIV).

And should our Lord make you a truly discerning Christian, do ask Him to help you wrap that discernment in a protective covering of love.

Clearly, the more loving you are, the more discerning you are certain to be.

---

1.   Foster, *Third View of Tongues*, p. 110.
2.   _____ , *Revolution of Love.*

Epilogue

After this text was completed, I had occasion to come in contact once again with the ministry of a Christian brother whom I know to be one of the most discerning men in the kingdom.

I was struck again by his simplicity, his love, his openness, even his credulity. There was no hint of cynicism, no attitude of negativism, no bent toward suspicion.

And I could not help but think, "Here is a man of God, truly discerning, who expresses love, who believes all things, who exemplifies all that I have been trying to say."

I liked what I saw. Love and openness do make all the difference.

Bibliography

Blamires, Harry. *The Christian Mind.* Ann Arbor: Servant Books, 1978.

Bruce, F. F. *The Book of Acts.* Grand Rapids: Eerdmans Publishing Company, 1956.

Buckles, Peter. "What Are Christian College Students Like?" *Christianity Today,* November 2, 1979.

Clark, Gordon H. *A Christian View of Men and Things.* Grand Rapids: Eerdmans Publishing Company, 1954.

Elliot, Elisabeth. *Let Me Be a Woman.* Wheaton: Tyndale House Publishers, 1976.

Falwell, Jerry. *Listen America!* Garden City: Doubleday and Company, 1980.

Foster, K. Neill. *Revolution of Love.* Minneapolis: Bethany Fellowship, 1973.

_____ . *The Third View of Tongues.* Minneapolis: Bethany Fellowship, 1975.

Jewett, Paul K. *Man as Male and Female.* Grand Rapids: Eerdmans Publishing Company, 1975.

Johnston, Arthur P. *The Battle for World Evangelism.* Wheaton: Tyndale House Publishers, 1978.

Lenski, R.C.H. *The Acts of the Apostles.* Minneapolis: Augsburg Publishing Company, 1944.

Lindsell, Harold. *Battle for the Bible.* Grand Rapids: Zondervan Publishing Company, 1976.

McLead, Wilburt. *Charismatic or Christian*. Saskatoon: Western Tract Mission, 1978.

Mounce, Robert H. "The Marks of an Educated Man" *Christianity Today*, November 2, 1979.

Nevius, John L. *Demon Possession*. Grand Rapids: Kregel Publications, 1968.

Orr, James. *The Christian View of God and the World*. Grand Rapids: Eerdmans Publishing Company, 1954.

Quebedeaux, Richard. *The Worldly Evangelicals*. New York: Harper and Row, Publishers, 1978.

Rogers, Jack, ed. *Biblical Authority*. Waco: Word Books, 1977.

Stott, John R. W. *Christian Mission*. Downers Grove: InterVarsity Press, 1975.

Strong, James. *Hebrew and Chaldee Dictionary*. New York: Abingdon Press, 1890.

Tozer, A.W. *The Menace of the Religious Movie*. Harrisburg: Christian Publications, Inc.